THIS BIBLE STUDY JOURNAL BELONGS TO:

Seek the *Lord* and his *strength*;
seek his *presence* continually!

1 CHRONICLES 16:11 (ESV)

52 Weeks in the Word

YOUR GUIDE FOR READING THE BIBLE CAREFULLY, STUDYING IT PRAYERFULLY & LIVING IT OUT PRACTICALLY

KAREN EHMAN
RUTH SCHWENK
COURTNEY JOSEPH

All Scripture quotations, unless otherwise indicated, are taken from the Holy Bible, New International Version®, NIV®. Copyright ©1973, 1978, 1984, 2011 by Biblica, Inc.™ Used by permission of Zondervan. All rights reserved worldwide. www.zondervan.com The "NIV" and "New International Version" are trademarks registered in the United States Patent and Trademark Office by Biblica, Inc.™

Scripture quotations marked AMP are taken from the Amplified® Bible. Copyright © 1954, 1958, 1962, 1964, 1965, 1987, 2015 by The Lockman Foundation. Used by permission. (www.Lockman.org).

Scripture quotations marked CEV are taken from the Contemporary English Version. Copyright © 1991, 1992, 1995 by American Bible Society. Used by permission.

Scripture quotations marked CSB® are taken from the Christian Standard Bible®, Copyright © 2017 by Holman Bible Publishers. Used by permission. Christian Standard Bible®, and CSB®, are federally registered trademarks of Holman Bible Publishers.

Scripture quotations marked ESV are taken from the ESV® Bible (The Holy Bible, English Standard Version®). Copyright © 2001 by Crossway, a publishing ministry of Good News Publishers. Used by permission. All rights reserved.

Scripture quotations marked NASB are taken from the New American Standard Bible®. Copyright © 1960, 1962, 1963, 1968, 1971, 1972, 1973, 1975, 1977, 1995 by The Lockman Foundation. Used by permission. (www.Lockman.org).

Scripture quotations marked NLT are taken from the Holy Bible, New Living Translation. © 1996, 2004, 2015 by Tyndale House Foundation. Used by permission of Tyndale House Publishers, Inc., Carol Stream, Illinois 60188. All rights reserved.

Any internet addresses (websites, blogs, etc.) in this book are offered as a resource. They are not intended in any way to be or imply an endorsement by the authors, nor do the authors vouch for the content of these sites and numbers for the life of this book.

No part of this publication may be reproduced, stored in a retrieval system, or transmitted in any form or by any means—electronic, mechanical, photocopy, recording, or any other—except for brief quotations in printed reviews, without the prior permission of the authors.

Hi Friend,

We are so thrilled that you have purchased our study resource *52 Weeks in the Word*. It is our deepest desire and most sincere prayer that it will help you to develop a consistent time of connecting with God through his Word each week. We know carving out space in your schedule can be difficult. No matter your stage of life or what season you find yourself in, extra time in your day is hard to find. Our prayer is that you will make such a time a doable priority because you have a resource that will help you along the way.

May the next 52 weeks be a time of sweet fellowship with Jesus and may you see the fruit of your study in your relationships, your responsibilities, and in your spiritual life.

Know that we are cheering you on in your relationship with the Lord and we are walking along side of you too.

In His Endless Love,

Karen, Courtney, and Ruth

HOW TO USE THIS
BIBLE STUDY GUIDE

This resource is meant to be used over a 52-week span as you read each passage of the week carefully, study it prayerfully, and live it out practically. Each week there is a four-page spread that includes the following:

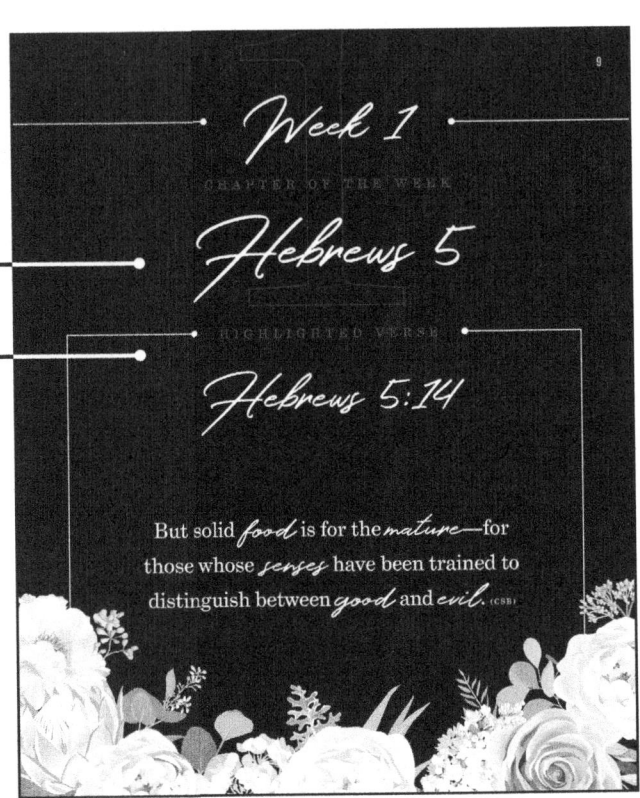

Scripture to Study

This section includes the **chapter of the week**, and a **highlighted verse or verses** that will be explored for deeper study.

Read it Carefully

Here you will **write out the verse** for yourself and then circle or highlight any key words. Also **jot down initial thoughts** you have about the scripture.

It also gives you a few **other corresponding scriptures** on the same or a related topic.

Study it Prayerfully

Each week this section contains content meant to help clarify the meaning of the scripture with **commentary and also the biblical context**. There is also a call out portion that highlights the Hebrew or Greek meaning of a word in the passage that helps to make the original intended meaning come alive more than it does in the English transliteration.

Finally, there is a **"My Prayer to God"** section where a prayer prompt is provided to enable you craft a personal prayer on the topic of the passage being studied.

Live it Out Practically

This section **repeats the highlighted verse** of the week again and also contains **a few practical application questions** to ponder. It is meant to help you implement the directives discovered in your study into your everyday life and relationships.

There is also a **"Where I Saw God Today"** blank bordered section to record how you saw God working in your life that week, or to list something you are thankful for.

Finally, there is a second blank bordered section entitled **"Where I Need God Today"** where you may jot down a prayer request or two, petitioning help from the Lord.

Week 1

CHAPTER OF THE WEEK

Hebrews 5

HIGHLIGHTED VERSE

Hebrews 5:14

But solid *food* is for the *mature*—for those whose *senses* have been trained to distinguish between *good* and *evil*. (CSB)

Read it *Carefully*

Related *Verses*

Wisdom is supreme—so get wisdom. And whatever else you get, get understanding.

PROVERBS 4:7 (CSB)

Pay careful attention, then, to how you walk—not as unwise people but as wise— making the most of the time, because the days are evil.

EPHESIANS 5:15-16 (CSB)

Don't stifle the Spirit. Don't despise prophecies but test all things. Hold on to what is good. Stay away from every kind of evil.

1 THESSALONIANS 5:19-22 (CSB)

Study it *Prayerfully*

IN HEBREWS CHAPTER 5, the author addresses the constant practice needed by believers to sharpen our spiritual skills and gain the power of discernment to distinguish good from evil. Often in this epistle, the language is encouraging. Here, however, the tone is somewhat scolding as the recipients are rebuked for their lack of maturity.

It does not seem that the believers in this audience are recent converts considered to be "baby Christians." Hebrews 5:12 even asserts that they should already be exhibiting a faith deep enough to position them to instruct others: "For though by this time you ought to be teachers..." The author of Hebrews recommends a refresher course in the basics of the faith for his readers. These spiritual fundamentals are described as "... the basic principles of the oracles of God." Then they are summed up with one simple word: milk.

Just as infants eventually transition from ingesting only milk to eating solid foods as their bodies grow and their needs change, followers of Christ are to "grow up" in their faith, both in learning and in practice. Such growth occurs as we acquire both information and experience, sharpening our spiritual skills and becoming mature and able to move on to solid food.

Have you graduated to a diet of solid spiritual food? This is a sign of maturity in the Lord.

—*Karen*

> *The Greek term for our English word "mature" in Hebrews 5:14 is* **teleios** *(pronounced* tel'-i-os*) and it is translated as "perfect." Not perfect as in without flaw or sin, but in the sense of being complete, whole or in full form. Such a mature believer is better positioned to distinguish good from evil.*

MY **PRAYER** TO GOD

Dear Father, a place in my life where I need spiritual maturity is . . .

_____
_____
_____
_____
_____
_____

Live it Out *Practically*

Hebrews 5:14

But solid food is for the mature—for those whose senses have been trained to distinguish between good and evil. (CSB)

APPLICATION QUESTIONS

The constant and consistent practice of our faith gives God fertile ground where His Holy Word can be planted. (James 1:21) This results in a strong believer who is more effective not only in practicing discernment but also in sharing the gospel, bringing others into the fold who will also start with milk but will eventually move on to maturity in the faith. (1 Corinthians 3:5-7)

In what ways are you currently being intentional about your spiritual growth?

If you aren't, is there an action step you might take to position yourself to more effectively mature in your faith?

Where I *Saw* God today

Where I *Need* God today

Week 2

CHAPTER OF THE WEEK

Psalm 62

HIGHLIGHTED VERSE

Psalm 62:1

Truly my soul finds *rest in God;* my *salvation* comes from him.

Read it *Carefully*

Related

Be still before the Lord and wait patiently for him; do not fret when people succeed in their ways, when they carry out their wicked schemes.

PSALM 37:7

This is what the Lord says: "When seventy years are completed for Babylon, I will come to you and fulfill my good promise to bring you back to this place. For I know the plans I have for you," declares the Lord, "plans to prosper you and not to harm you, plans to give you hope and a future. Then you will call on me and come and pray to me, and I will listen to you. You will seek me and find me when you seek me with all your heart.

JEREMIAH 29:10-13

Study it *Prayerfully*

ARE YOU IN A SEASON OF WAITING AND WONDERING? In Psalm 62:1, the Psalmist is declaring his trust in God in the middle of what must be a waiting season because just a few verses later, in verse 3, he cries out in his distress, "how long?" We can assume this isn't something new but rather a place he has found himself in for a while.

The stress of waiting can be crushing, and we can wonder if God will ever answer our prayers or come through in the way we hope. But I love how the Psalmist follows the pattern we see so often in the Psalms, which is a complaint, a petition, and then a declaration.

This declaration in Psalm 62:1 is a reminder that no matter what we are going through, we can wait with patience, and we can trust Him with confidence. We don't need to move ahead of God. We can take our stress to Him, and we will find rest in Him.

—*Ruth*

> *The Hebrew word for "wait" or "rest" in Psalm 62:1 is* **dumiya** *(pronounced* doo-me-yaw*). It means to be quiet or still in waiting.*

MY **PRAYER** TO GOD

Lord, I want to trust You fully as I wait and wonder about . . .

_____
_____
_____
_____
_____

Live it Out *Practically*

Psalm 62:1
Truly my soul finds rest in God; my salvation comes from him.

APPLICATION QUESTIONS

In what areas of life do you find it most difficult to wait? List any that pop into your mind.

How does understanding the rest God offers change the way we wait?

What shift in perspective or in thinking does it cause for you?

Where I *Saw* God today

Where I *Need* God today

Week 3

CHAPTER OF THE WEEK

Psalm 119

HIGHLIGHTED VERSE

Psalm 119:11

I have *hidden your word* in my heart that I might *not sin against you.*

Read it *Carefully*

Related *Verses*

All Scripture is God-breathed and is useful for teaching, rebuking, correcting, and training in righteousness, so that the servant of God may be thoroughly equipped for every good work.

2 Timothy 3:16-17

The unfolding of your words gives light; it gives understanding to the simple.

Psalm 119:130

Your word is a lamp for my feet, a light on my path.

Psalm 119:105

Study it *Prayerfully*

IN THE OVERWHELM OF LIFE and all the daily busyness we face, we can so easily forget what really fuels us and gives us direction. More than a cup of coffee, a good workout, or an easy life, we need God's Word. It is what strengthens us and sustains us, no matter what a day holds. Psalm 119:11 reminds us that God's Word guards our hearts and keeps us from sin.

The Hebrew for "sin" has the meaning of "to miss." To miss what? To miss the mark of what God has commanded us. But it also has the meaning "to miss" the life God wants for us! I love that!

God's Word brings hope, and it brings clarity to the way we walk out our days. God wants good for us, and He has good for us when we walk faithfully in obedience to His Word. How do we treasure and store God's Word in our hearts? By knowing it. We pray, worship, memorize, meditate on it, read it, and cling to it. God's Word gives us strength and protects us as we feed on it day after day.

—*Ruth*

> *The Hebrew word in Psalm 119:11 for "hidden" is* **sapan** *(pronounced* tsaw-fan*). It means to hide, treasure, or store up.*

MY **PRAYER** TO **GOD**

Lord Jesus, I want to hide Your word in my heart so I might fully follow You and . . .

___
___
___
___
___
___

Live it Out *Practically*

Psalm 119:11

I have hidden your word in my heart that I might not sin against you.

APPLICATION QUESTIONS

In what ways could you begin to hide God's Word in your heart? List any methods you can think of here.

Now, how will you implement this goal moving forward? Circle one way you listed above that you will begin to focus on.

Where I *Saw* God today

Where I *Need* God today

Week 4

CHAPTER OF THE WEEK

Psalm 46

HIGHLIGHTED VERSE

Psalm 46:10

He says, "Be *still*, and *know* that I am *God*; I will be *exalted* among the nations, I will be exalted in the *earth*."

Read it *Carefully*

Related

Be still before the Lord and wait patiently for him; do not fret when people succeed in their ways, when they carry out their wicked schemes.

PSALM 37:7

The Lord will fight for you; you need only to be still.

EXODUS 14:14

He got up, rebuked the wind and said to the waves, "Quiet! Be still!" Then the wind died down and it was completely calm. He said to his disciples, "Why are you so afraid? Do you still have no faith?" They were terrified and asked each other, "Who is this? Even the wind and the waves obey him!"

MARK 4:39-41

Study it *Prayerfully*

PSALM 46:1 SAYS that God is our refuge and strength, a very present help in times of trouble. Strength does not require God plus something or someone else. God alone is to be our refuge and strength. He is with us!

So often, we try to face battles on our own. We fret and scheme, trying to obtain a certain outcome rather than quietly releasing our situation to God, trusting him to take care of it while we remain still.

When we are still, that is when we can truly reflect and know that God is with us. And when we know God is with us, we experience his peace. In the midst of our trials, we can rest in knowing that the God of Israel and heavenly hosts has it all under control.

Now today, determine that you will be still, release it to God and put your trust in him.

—*Courtney*

> *The Hebrew word for "still" in Psalm 46:10 is* **rapha** *(pronounced raw-faw'). It means to be weak, let go, or release.*

MY **PRAYER** TO **GOD**

Father God, I need to experience Your peace in my life in the area of . . .

_____
_____
_____
_____
_____
_____
_____

Live it Out *Practically*

Psalm 46:10
Be still and know that I am God.

APPLICATION **QUESTIONS**

Why do you think it is sometimes hard for you to be still and trust God to be in control——to be weak, let go, or release something to Jesus?

What is stealing your peace today? Briefly describe it here below.

How can the truth of Psalm 46:1 help you deal with this situation going forward?

Where I *Saw* God today	Where I *Need* God today

Week 5

CHAPTER OF THE WEEK

Philippians 1

HIGHLIGHTED VERSE

Philippians 1:12

I want you to know, *brothers*, that what has happened to me has really served to *advance the gospel.* (ESV)

Read it *Carefully*

Related *Verses*

God is our refuge and strength, a helper who is always found in times of trouble.

Psalm 46:1 (CSB)

Blessed be the Lord, for he has heard the sound of my pleading. The Lord is my strength and my shield; my heart trusts in him, and I am helped. Therefore my heart celebrates, and I give thanks to him with my song.

Psalm 28:6-7 (CSB)

You rejoice in this, even though now for a short time, if necessary, you suffer grief in various trials so that the proven character of your faith—more valuable than gold which, though perishable, is refined by fire—may result in praise, glory, and honor at the revelation of Jesus Christ.

1 Peter 1:6-7 (CSB)

Study it *Prayerfully*

I LOVE THE WAY PAUL FLIPS THE SCRIPT and reframes his time in prison in the letter of Philippians. He doesn't complain about his incarceration in a lonely, dingy prison cell. Instead, he rejoices in the progress being made in the eternal realm. What was meant to handcuff him physically was not able to shackle him spiritually. His prison became a platform where he could spread the Good News about Jesus.

Those nearest in proximity physically to Paul heard the gospel: the imperial guard. But the news of the gospel of Jesus didn't stop there. The phrase "and to all the rest" shows the multiplying effect that occurred, ensuring even more people heard the salvation story.

Others were emboldened when they saw Paul use his chains as an invitation to preach. His Philippian friends weren't reading a letter from a bewildered and panicked person questioning, "What has happened to me?" Those same words became a calm and insightful statement instead: "... what has happened to me has really served to advance the gospel."

Paul's prison became his platform and others saw Jesus through his hard season of life.

—*Karen*

> *The Greek word for "advance" in Philippians 1:12 is* **prokopé** *(pronounced* prok-op-ay'*) and its definition is to make progress, to gain furtherance, or to turn a profit.*

MY **PRAYER** TO **GOD**

Dear God, I want my hard times to be an opportunity for me to point others to You. Help me to ...

Live it Out *Practically*

Philippians 1:12

I want you to know, brothers, that what has happened to me has really served to advance the gospel. (ESV)

APPLICATION **QUESTIONS**

Many of us find ourselves in situations that feel confining. We might feel stuck in a job, a hard relationship or even a physical disability or illness that limits us. Let Paul's example spark your own faith, prompting you to cry out to God. Not, "Lord, please get me out of here!" But rather, "Father, why have you brought me here?" The answer is the same one given to Paul: so that others will see and hear the gospel through you.

In what ways do you feel imprisoned in your life? Write any thoughts that come to mind.

How might what you see as your current prison become a platform to point others to the Lord?

Where I *Saw* God today

Where I *Need* God today

Week 6

CHAPTER OF THE WEEK

Romans 8

HIGHLIGHTED VERSE

Romans 8:6

The mind governed by the flesh is death, but the mind governed by the Spirit is life and peace.

Read it *Carefully*

Related *Verses*

Finally, brothers and sisters, whatever is true, whatever is noble, whatever is right, whatever is pure, whatever is lovely, whatever is admirable—if anything is excellent or praiseworthy—think about such things.

PHILIPPIANS 4:8

Do not conform to the pattern of this world, but be transformed by the renewing of your mind. Then you will be able to test and approve what God's will is—his good, pleasing and perfect will.

ROMANS 12:2

You will keep in perfect peace those whose minds are steadfast, because they trust in you.

ISAIAH 26:3

Study it *Prayerfully*

I AM THE FIRST ONE TO ADMIT that I can struggle to keep my mind and thoughts under control. Worry creeps in too often, and I find myself going down ridiculous rabbit trails of what-ifs. There is a reason the Bible speaks so often about keeping our minds renewed and our thoughts under control. It is hard work, and it matters. Romans 8:6 tells us that "the mind governed by the flesh is death." Yikes! Those rabbit trails can lead to despair and destruction.

Our thoughts indeed have an impact on us, but the good news is that there is hope! Romans 8:6 also tells us that we don't have to live in the land of what-ifs because God offers us something better. We can surrender every thought to His power and presence, and when we do this, we can experience life and peace. We might say to have peace is to be absent of chaos! In essence, we have a rich spiritual life and future in Christ when we let the Spirit control our minds and guard our thoughts with the truth of the Gospel.

The key to remember here is that the power to change our thinking doesn't come from us. It is the Holy Spirit working in us. When we surrender our wandering minds to Him, He is faithful to correct our thinking and give us His peace instead.

—*Ruth*

> *The word "life" in Greek is* **zoe** *(pronounced* dzo-ay*). It means both physical (present) and spiritual (particularly future) existence and vitality. And the word "peace" in Greek is* **eiréné** *(pronounced* i-ray'-nay*) and it means tranquility, prosperity, and harmony.*

MY **PRAYER** TO **GOD**

Heavenly Father, please empower me to change my thinking in the area of . . .

_____
_____
_____
_____
_____
_____

Live it Out *Practically*

Romans 8:6

The mind governed by the flesh is death, but the mind governed by the Spirit is life and peace.

APPLICATION **QUESTIONS**

What area of your thought life do you need to surrender to God the most right now? Write it out below.

How can you replace the wrong thoughts with a mind that is focused on the things of God? Read Philippians 4:8 here in the AMP version of the Bible before giving your answer: *Finally, believers, whatever is true, whatever is honorable and worthy of respect, whatever is right and confirmed by God's word, whatever is pure and wholesome, whatever is lovely and brings peace, whatever is admirable and of good repute; if there is any excellence, if there is anything worthy of praise, think continually on these things [center your mind on them, and implant them in your heart].*

Where I *Saw* God today

Where I *Need* God today

Week 7

CHAPTER OF THE WEEK

Matthew 22

HIGHLIGHTED VERSES

Matthew 22:37-38

Jesus replied: "'Love the Lord your God with all your *heart* and with all your *soul* and with all your *mind*.' This is the first and *greatest commandment*."

Read it *Carefully*

Related *Verses*

And now, Israel, what does the Lord your God ask of you but to fear the Lord your God, to walk in obedience to him, to love him, to serve the Lord your God with all your heart and with all your soul.

DEUTERONOMY 10:12

Love the Lord your God with all your heart and with all your soul and with all your mind and with all your strength.'

MARK 12:30

He answered, "'Love the Lord your God with all your heart and with all your soul and with all your strength and with all your mind'; and, 'Love your neighbor as yourself.'"

LUKE 10:27

Study it *Prayerfully*

JESUS SAID THE FIRST AND GREATEST COMMANDMENT is to love God with all of our heart, soul and mind. This includes all of our thoughts and feelings. Is there something or someone who competes with God for your love?

If we put the things of this world before God, we will regret it when we see God face to face. Everything we put before God from this world ends at the grave. We can't take our money, success, clothes, house, degree, or anything else from this world with us into eternity.

God wants us to enjoy life! But he does not want us to turn the enjoyable and good things in our lives into little gods that we give all of our time, attention and love to, instead of him. Let's be determined to keep first things first—the Lord God himself.

—*Courtney*

> *The Greek word for "heart" in Matthew 22:37-38 is* **kardia** *(pronounced kar-dee'-ah). The root word of kardia is* kar *which means heart. The entire word together means the thoughts and feelings of the human heart.*

MY PRAYER TO GOD

Dear Lord, I don't want my affections for the things of this world to be greater than my love for You. Help me to . . .

_____
_____
_____
_____
_____
_____

Live it Out *Practically*

Matthew 22:37-38

Jesus replied: "'Love the Lord your God with all your heart and with all your soul and with all your mind.' This is the first and greatest commandment."

APPLICATION QUESTIONS

Let's take an honest inventory of our thoughts and feelings today. Be completely truthful. Is there anything or anyone competing with God for your love? Write it out below.

How can the words of Matthew 22:37-38 help to align your thinking with God's ways when it comes to the situation you mentioned? What will you do differently going forward?

Where I *Saw* God today

Where I *Need* God today

Week 8

CHAPTER OF THE WEEK

Matthew 22

HIGHLIGHTED VERSE

Matthew 22:39

"And the second is like it: 'Love your neighbor as yourself.'"

Read it *Carefully*

Related *Verses*

So in everything, do to others what you would have them do to you, for this sums up the Law and the Prophets.

MATTHEW 7:12

Let no debt remain outstanding, except the continuing debt to love one another, for whoever loves others has fulfilled the law. The commandments, "You shall not commit adultery," "You shall not murder," "You shall not steal," "You shall not covet," and whatever other command there may be, are summed up in this one command: "Love your neighbor as yourself." Love does no harm to a neighbor. Therefore, love is the fulfillment of the law.

ROMANS 13:8-10

My command is this: Love each other as I have loved you.

JOHN 15:12

Study it *Prayerfully*

WE ALL LOVE OURSELVES, so Jesus' command to love our neighbor is based on our natural love of self. We all have a drive inside of us to be happy and think of ourselves first. No one has to teach a 2-year-old to be selfish. It is their natural default.

Notice that this is not a command to stop loving ourselves or to stop having needs that need met. Instead, Jesus says to love your neighbor AS yourself. The key word is "as." In the same unstoppable way that you feed yourself, seek to be loved, or seek comfort, you should purpose to love, feed, and comfort others. You tend to your own physical and emotional needs. We should make sure these needs are met too in the lives of those we connect with each week.

As you interact with the many people you encounter in your life this week, remember the words of Matthew 22:39. May the degree of our self-seeking be to the degree of our self-giving.

—Courtney

> *The Greek word for "neighbor" is* **plésion** *(pronounced play-see'-on). Pelas means near and plesion means a friend or fellow nearby.*

MY **PRAYER** TO **GOD**

Almighty God, I want to love my neighbors as myself. This week, help me to . . .

_____
_____
_____
_____
_____
_____

Live it Out *Practically*

Matthew 22:39

"And the second is like it: 'Love your neighbor as yourself.'"

APPLICATION **QUESTIONS**

Is there someone you need to love better? Perhaps a friend, a spouse, a child, a co-worker, a neighbor or even an enemy? Name that person that comes to mind.

Now, spend some time asking the Lord to give you more love for that person.

Where I *Saw* God today

Where I *Need* God today

Week 9

CHAPTER OF THE WEEK

Jonah 1

HIGHLIGHTED VERSE

Jonah 1:3

But Jonah rose to flee to Tarshish from the *presence* of the LORD. He went down to Joppa and found a *ship* going to Tarshish. So he paid the fare and went down into it, to go with them to Tarshish, away from the *presence* of the LORD. (ESV)

Read it *Carefully*

Related *Verses*

You are my friends if you keep on doing what I command you.

JOHN 15:14 (AMP)

This is love: that we walk according to his commands. This is the command as you have heard it from the beginning: that you walk in love.

2 JOHN 1:6 (CSB)

He said, "Rather, blessed are those who hear the word of God and keep it."

LUKE 11:28 (CSB)

Study it *Prayerfully*

IN THE BOOK OF JONAH, we see the prophet making an intentional choice to move away from God. Jonah had been told by God to go to the great city of Nineveh, which was part of the Assyrian Empire. But instead of moving toward God's will for him, Jonah did an about-face and headed far away from God's plan for him both geographically and spiritually.

Nineveh was on the eastern bank of the Tigris river, which is about 220 miles north of present-day Baghdad. It was an important ("great") city (Jonah 3:3) However, the Ninevites did not serve the Lord.

Jonah had no interest in preaching to the wicked inhabitants of Nineveh. And so he made a mad dash instead to Tarshish. However, we aren't told until a few chapters later the explanation for his decision to disobey God. He was aware of God's compassion and forgiving character, but in spite of being a sinner himself and a recipient of God's grace, Jonah had no desire for God to grant pardon to the inhabitants of Nineveh. (Jonah 4:2) This caused him to move away from God's will for him.

—*Karen*

> *The Hebrew word for "flee" in Jonah 1:3,* **barach** *(pronounced baw-rakh') means to put into flight or to move hurriedly away from.*

MY PREVAYER TO GOD

Gracious Father, right now in life I want to run away from . . .

_____
_____
_____
_____
_____
_____

Live it Out *Practically*

Jonah 1:3

But Jonah rose to flee to Tarshish from the presence of the LORD. He went down to Joppa and found a ship going to Tarshish. So he paid the fare and went down into it, to go with them to Tarshish, away from the presence of the LORD. (ESV)

APPLICATION QUESTIONS

Today, when God calls us to follow His Word—the commands of Scripture—what will we do? Will we draw closer to Him in obedience, or will we, like Jonah, run away from His presence? At those times when we don't enjoy a closeness to God, maybe we should ask ourselves: "Who moved?"

When you think about your own closeness to the Lord, do you feel that in any way you have moved away from God? If so, how did this happen?

If there is a situation in your life which you know has caused you to move away from the Lord and his will, how will you correct that behavior today?

Where I *Saw* God today

Where I *Need* God today

Week 10

CHAPTER OF THE WEEK

Proverbs 31

HIGHLIGHTED VERSE

Proverbs 31:25

> She is clothed with *strength* and *dignity*; she can *laugh* at the days to come.

Read it *Carefully*

Related *Verses*

You will laugh at destruction and famine, and need not fear the wild animals.

JOB 5:22

The LORD is my light and my salvation— whom shall I fear? The LORD is the stronghold of my life— of whom shall I be afraid?

PSALM 27:1

They will have no fear of bad news; their hearts are steadfast, trusting in the Lord.

PSALM 112:7

Study it *Prayerfully*

THERE IS PLENTY TO WORRY ABOUT in today's world. Whether it is a personal health diagnosis, a wayward child, financial struggles, or a strained relationship, the many things we face can threaten our peace and joy.

The book of Proverbs describes a woman who, although her life wasn't perfect, was a person of character who can "laugh at the days to come." She wasn't overcome with worry and weariness or worn out from all that she had to do, but rather she laughed. Sometimes I can forget to laugh, actually many times. I take the job of today so seriously that I can't find the time to stop and enjoy it, or I'm consumed (rightfully so) with the struggles of life, and joy seems nowhere to be found. But the Proverbs 31 woman laughed, and it wasn't just a shallow kind of joy you may think of when you think of laughing; she laughed because she trusted that God was in control.

In the Hebrew language, "she can laugh" means a mocking type of laugh, to make sport or to jest. It is almost like a dare at the days to come. That is the kind of laughing I want to experience. Laughter that stems from a heart that isn't afraid of tomorrow and dares to have joy and hope because God is completely sovereign and can be trusted with every detail.

—Ruth

> *The strength spoken of in Proverbs 31:25 in the Hebrew language is **oz** (pronounced oze) and is strength not of body, but of mind. The woman here is strong in moral character; vigorous and honorable.*

MY **PRAYER** TO **GOD**

Dear Lord, I need moral strength in character in the area of . . .

_____
_____
_____
_____
_____
_____
_____

Live it Out *Practically*

Proverbs 31:25

She is clothed with strength and dignity;
she can laugh at the days to come.

APPLICATION QUESTIONS

When you think of the future, does it make you want to laugh or to cry? List any areas that make you laugh and others that make you feel like crying.

Now, knowing that you can laugh at the days to come because God is in control, confidently copy this sentence below, adding in any area where you feel more like crying:

Father God, I trust You. Because of this, I can laugh at the days to come when I think of _____.

Where I *Saw* God today

Where I *Need* God today

Week 11

CHAPTER OF THE WEEK

Matthew 11

HIGHLIGHTED VERSE

Matthew 11:28

"Come to me, all you who are *weary* and *burdened*, and I will give you *rest*."

Read it *Carefully*

Related *Verses*

In peace I will lie down and sleep, for you alone, Lord, make me dwell in safety.

Psalm 4:8

The Lord is my shepherd, I lack nothing. He makes me lie down in green pastures, he leads me beside quiet waters.

Psalm 23:1-2

Whoever dwells in the shelter of the Most High will rest in the shadow of the Almighty. I will say of the Lord, "He is my refuge and my fortress, my God, in whom I trust."

Psalm 91:1-2

Study it *Prayerfully*

DID YOU KNOW that the Chinese pictograph for the word "busy" is two characters: a heart and killing? Isn't that appropriate? The clock ticks fast everyday as I move from breakfast to lunch to dinner and then back to breakfast once again. The calendar pages flip fast and before I know it, we are saying "Happy New Year" once again!

And there at the end of the year, as I'm exhausted from holiday expectations ... I feel it ... the heart killing. And so, hope is restored on January 1st, when the slate feels clean and a new year begins. The idea of a second chance to slow down, rework my priorities and live well begins ... but inevitably, by March, I'm defeated. I have done it again. I have made myself too busy again. I am just so tired ... again.

Are you tired? Jesus says, "Come to me." Then he promises, "and I will give you rest."

God holds rest out to us. It is available. All we have to do is slow down and accept his rest as a good gift because the secret to finding rest is found in Jesus.

—*Courtney*

> *The Greek word for "rest" in Matthew 11:28 is* **anapano** *(pronounced* anapauō*). Anapano means to be refreshed, to take it easy, or to relax.*

MY **PRAYER** TO **GOD**

Dear God, I need Your rest in my life because I am weary and burdened about ...

_____
_____
_____
_____
_____
_____

Live it Out *Practically*

Matthew 11:28

Come to me, all you who are weary and burdened, and I will give you rest.

APPLICATION **QUESTIONS**

Are you tired? List all of the aspects of your current life that are making you physically weary.

What is making you mentally weary and burdened today? List those items here also.

I know your heart needs rest. Take your burdens to the Lord in prayer and give it all to him. He loves you and will help you to carry your heavy load.

Where I *Saw* God today

Where I *Need* God today

Week 12

CHAPTER OF THE WEEK

Genesis 1

HIGHLIGHTED VERSES

Genesis 1:1-2

In the *beginning* God created the *heavens* and the *earth*. Now the earth was formless and empty, darkness was over the surface of the deep, and the *Spirit of God* was hovering over the waters.

Read it *Carefully*

Related *Verses*

Yours, Lord, is the greatness and the power and the glory and the majesty and the splendor, for everything in heaven and earth is yours. Yours, Lord, is the kingdom; you are exalted as head over all.

1 Chronicles 29:11

For even if there are so-called gods, whether in heaven or on earth (as indeed there are many "gods" and many "lords"), yet for us there is but one God, the Father, from whom all things came and for whom we live; and there is but one Lord, Jesus Christ, through whom all things came and through whom we live.

1 Corinthians 8:5-6

Study it *Prayerfully*

IT IS NO SECRET that the Bible testifies over and over to the power and majesty of God. But did you know that the names used for God throughout the Bible have all different meanings to speak of who he is?

Starting here at the very beginning of the Bible, we see the name Elohim used for God. Elohim is the first name for God used in the Bible, and it speaks to his majesty and strength. In fact, Elohim is used more than two thousand times throughout the Bible and thirty-two times here in Genesis 1 alone.

I love that the Bible starts with a reminder for us of how powerful our God is. He is sovereign over our lives, and there is nothing we face that is too hard for him. Whatever you are facing today, you are not alone. He is our powerful King over all of creation, and that includes every detail of your life today. You can trust our Creator, friend.

—*Ruth*

> *The term* **Elohim** *(pronounced el-o-heem') is plural in Genesis 1:1 and has been thought by many scholars to refer to the plurality of the Godhead—the Father, Son, and Spirit.*

MY **PRAYER** TO **GOD**

Father God, I need to remember that You are Elohim in the area of . . .

_____
_____
_____
_____
_____
_____

Live it Out *Practically*

Genesis 1:1-2

In the beginning, God created the heavens and the earth. Now the earth was formless and empty, darkness was over the surface of the deep, and the Spirit of God was hovering over the waters.

APPLICATION QUESTIONS

Elohim is the first name for God used in the Bible, and it speaks to his majesty and strength. What circumstance in your life do you need to hand over to God and remember that he is Elohim?

How can this week's highlighted verse help you to do so?

Where I *Saw* God today	Where I *Need* God today

Week 13

CHAPTER OF THE WEEK

Acts 7

HIGHLIGHTED VERSE

Acts 7:60

He *knelt down* and *cried out* with a loud voice, "Lord, do not hold this sin against them!" And after saying this, *he fell asleep.* (CSB)

Read it *Carefully*

Related *Verses*

And be kind and compassionate to one another, forgiving one another, just as God also forgave you] in Christ.

EPHESIANS 4:32 (CSB)

For if you forgive others their offenses, your heavenly Father will forgive you as well.

MATTHEW 6:14 (CSB)

Therefore, as God's chosen ones, holy and dearly loved, put on compassion, kindness, humility, gentleness, and patience—bearing with one another and forgiving one another if anyone has a grievance against another. Just as the Lord has forgiven you, so you are also to forgive.

COLOSSIANS 3:12-13 (CSB)

Study it *Prayerfully*

IN ACTS 7, we see Stephen recounting before the Sanhedrin in chronological order God's dealings with the nation of Israel. He speaks of Moses and Joseph and the way Israel rejected the leaders God had chosen. His speech comes to a climax when he talks about the ultimate rejection of Jesus in Acts 7:52. He accuses his listeners of being stiff-necked people, uncircumcised in both heart and ears who continually resisted the Holy Spirit, just as their forefathers did.

Enraged, the members of the Sanhedrin cut the speech short and grind their teeth. This image often described the action of God's enemies. (Luke 13:28; Job 16:9; Psalm 35:16) When they could stand it no longer, the listeners stoned Stephen to death.

However, before dying, Stephen gave us an astonishing example of the forgiveness offered through Jesus as he left this life praying for his killers, asking that their sin not be held against them. (Acts 7:60) His death was not in vain. It allowed the infant church to spread and ultimately grow in number and in faith.

— *Karen*

> *The Greek word in Acts 7:60 for "sin" is* **hamartia** *(pronounced ham-ar-tee'-ah) and it refers to one that occurs by omission or commission and can be in thought and feeling or in speech and by action.*

MY **PRAYER** TO **GOD**

Father, grow in me a heart like Stephen's. May I . . . .

_____
_____
_____
_____
_____
_____
_____

Live it Out *Practically*

Acts 7:60

He knelt down and cried out with a loud voice, "Lord, do not hold this sin against them!" And after saying this, he fell asleep. (CSB)

APPLICATION QUESTIONS

Is there someone in your life whom you are having a hard time forgiving? Write that person's name here.

What is it that they did to you to cause unforgiveness to well up in your heart?

How might the story of Stephen give you the conviction and courage to reach out in forgiveness to that person today?

Where I *Saw* God today

Where I *Need* God today

Week 14

CHAPTER OF THE WEEK

2 Corinthians 12

HIGHLIGHTED VERSES

2 Corinthians 12:8-9

Three times I *pleaded* with the Lord to take it away from me. But he said, "My *grace* is sufficient for you, for my *power* is made *perfect* in weakness."

Read it *Carefully*

Related *Verses*

That is why, for Christ's sake, I delight in weaknesses, in insults, in hardships, in persecutions, in difficulties. For when I am weak, then I am strong.

2 CORINTHIANS 12:10

In the same way, the Spirit helps us in our weakness. We do not know what we ought to pray for, but the Spirit himself intercedes for us through wordless groans.

ROMANS 8:26

Study it *Prayerfully*

WHEN MY FOUR KIDS WERE LITTLE, I felt like I was just doing my best to keep all the things together. One night I remember my son, Noah, dropping a small box of hard gumballs, and they all scattered across the hardwood floor, going this way and that. At that moment, I realized that my life felt a lot like those gumballs going everywhere. Whether it was a missing shoe, or we were running late to church, it seemed impossible to keep it all straight. I felt weak and wondered if I'd ever get it right.

Weakness isn't celebrated in our culture. We want to be strong, and have it all together or at least appear that way. But in the Bible, we see that our weakness has a purpose. Like Paul, we all have something that we wish God would take away. But in our weakness, God can change us and teach us to rely on Him.

God isn't waiting for us to have it all together. His glory shines brighter through our inadequacies and imperfections when we rely on His strength instead of our own. His power is made perfect in our weakness.

—*Ruth*

> *The Greek word for "perfected" is* **teleo** *(pronounced* tel-eh-o*), which means to finish, fulfill, and accomplish. In other words, Christ's miraculous power is fully upon us and accomplished in our weakness.*

MY **PRAYER** TO **GOD**

Creator God, I feel weak and need Your strength when it comes to . . .

_____
_____
_____
_____
_____
_____

Live it Out *Practically*

2 Corinthians 12:8-9

Three times I pleaded with the Lord to take it away from me. But he said, "My grace is sufficient for you, for my power is made perfect in weakness."

APPLICATION QUESTIONS

How is God asking you to embrace your weakness and rely on Him for the strength that you need?

What does that look like in your everyday life? List one way of thinking that will be different for you from now on.

Where I *Saw* God today

Where I *Need* God today

Week 15

CHAPTER OF THE WEEK

Psalm 90

HIGHLIGHTED VERSE

Psalm 90:14

Satisfy us in the morning with your unfailing *love*, that we may sing for *joy* and be *glad* all our days.

Read it *Carefully*

Related *Verses*

The LORD will guide you always; he will satisfy your needs in a sun-scorched land and will strengthen your frame. You will be like a well-watered garden, like a spring whose waters never fail.

ISAIAH 58:11

Let the morning bring me word of your unfailing love, for I have put my trust in you. Show me the way I should go, for to you I entrust my life.

PSALM 143:8

Because of the Lord's great love we are not consumed, for his compassions never fail. They are new every morning; great is your faithfulness.

LAMENTATIONS 3:22-23

Study it *Prayerfully*

THERE IS NO HOUR like the early morning hour to meet with God. Oftentimes we put off meeting with God until later in the day, but then our to-do list takes over and all day long we are chasing that quiet moment that does not exist. God does not want us chasing temporary things that do not satisfy us. Every morning he wants to satisfy us with his love.

The Bible does not command us to meet with God in the morning, but Jesus did! Many of the Old Testament men did too, like Abraham, Isaac, Jacob, Job, Moses, Joshua, Gideon, Samuel, David and many of the kings. We know that something powerful happens in the morning when men and women of God rise early in the morning and meet with him. Because it is in the morning that he satisfies us again with his love and gives us glad hearts that are strong for whatever the day may bring.

—*Courtney*

> *The Hebrew word for "satisfy" in Psalm 90:14 is* **saba** *(pronounced* saw-baw'*). Saba means to have enough or to be full and satisfied.*

MY **PRAYER** TO **GOD**

Heavenly Father, satisfy me with Your love. I want to . . .

_____
_____
_____
_____
_____
_____
_____

Live it Out *Practically*

Psalm 90:14

Satisfy us in the morning with your unfailing love, that we may sing for joy and be glad all our days.

APPLICATION QUESTIONS

It is humbling to admit that we need God every single morning, but we do, otherwise we spend the day seeking satisfaction in all the wrong places.

From whom or what do you tend to seek satisfaction?

How will you seek to satisfy yourself with God's word in the future after considering the words of Psalm 90:14?

Where I *Saw* God today

Where I *Need* God today

Week 16

CHAPTER OF THE WEEK

Psalm 18

HIGHLIGHTED VERSE

Psalm 18:28

For it is you who *light my lamp*; the LORD my God *lightens* my darkness. (ESV)

Read it *Carefully*

Related *Verses*

In the beginning God created the heavens and the earth.

GENESIS 1:1

When Jesus spoke again to the people, he said, "I am the light of the world. Whoever follows me will never walk in darkness, but will have the light of life."

JOHN 8:12

The light shines in the darkness, and the darkness has not overcome it.

JOHN 1:5

Study it *Prayerfully*

SOMETIMES LATE AT NIGHT, when I am struggling to sleep, I read a book on my Kindle. No matter how many times I've done it, as I open the e-reader, the light is always a bit startling at first. It isn't a bright light, but it doesn't have to be. Even just the soft glow of light has a way of illuminating the darkness. I don't even realize how dark it is until the light shines.

No matter how old we are, there are times in our lives when the darkness feels vast and heavy, and just a soft glow of light would make such a difference. The truth is that God doesn't leave us in our darkness. His light is there for us to see through it. When we are struggling to find our way in the middle of a hard season, we can trust that he is with us.

God gives us his Word, his promises, and his Son Jesus to light the way. We can stay close to him because, with him, we are never truly walking in darkness.

—*Ruth*

> *The word "light" in Hebrew is **or** (pronounced ore) and it means to shine or to become light. This doesn't just mean that there is a light, but that the Father is the light.*

MY **PRAYER** TO **GOD**

Heavenly Father, I need Your light in my life now when it comes to . . .

_____
_____
_____
_____
_____
_____
_____

Live it Out *Practically*

Psalm 18:28

For it is you who light my lamp;
the LORD my God lightens my darkness. (ESV)

APPLICATION **QUESTIONS**

What are some thoughts and feelings you might have about being somewhere strange and all alone in complete darkness? What might run through your mind?

When it comes to spiritual darkness, how can you stay close to God and experience his true light when you are walking through the darkness? Name one action step you will take this week to walk in his light.

Where I *Saw* God today

Where I *Need* God today

Week 17

CHAPTER OF THE WEEK

Galatians 1

HIGHLIGHTED VERSE

Galatians 1:6

I am *amazed* that you are so quickly turning away from him who *called* you by the *grace* of Christ and are *turning* to a different *gospel* . . . (CSB)

Read it *Carefully*

Related *Verses*

For I am not ashamed of the gospel, because it is the power of God for salvation to everyone who believes, first to the Jew, and also to the Greek.

ROMANS 1:16 (CSB

Then he said to them, "Go into all the world and preach the gospel to all creation.

MARK 16:15 (CSB

But not all obeyed the gospel. For Isaiah says, Lord, who has believed our message?

ROMANS 10:16 (CSB

Study it *Prayerfully*

AT THE BEGINNING OF PAUL'S LETTER to the Galatian church, we find him concerned about the church's ability to discern the true gospel from a counterfeit one that was circulating. Just what was this "different" gospel? While the original recipients of the letter may have understood what the apostle was talking about, to our modern eyes reading it, it might not be so clear.

The Christians in Galatia were being heavily influenced by a group of people known as the Judaizers whose views were in vast opposition to the gospel of Jesus. These men taught that to be a true believer, you must not only believe in Christ, but you also had to keep the law—namely circumcision and the ceremonial law—in order to be saved. By teaching this, they were adding to the gospel and changing the truth of believers being saved by grace alone. (Ephesians 2:8-9)

Worst of all, they caused some to embrace this different—and counterfeit—gospel.

As believers today, we need to make sure we are not adding requirements to the gospel; that we don't live as though Jesus + _____ (fill in the blank) equals salvation. Not a way to dress. Not a way to school our kids. Not a political party to support or a version of the Bible to use. Salvation is found through Jesus alone, not also through other behaviors we might add.

—*Karen*

> *In Greek, the word translated "different" is* **heteros** *(pronounced* het'-er-os*) and it refers to a second one, a contrastingly different variety, or the type of one's neighbor, rather than your own. It was also used in a military sense to mean to transfer your allegiance from your side to the enemies.*

MY PRAYER TO GOD

Almighty Father, may I not add anything to the gospel. When others look at my life, may they see . . .

_____
_____
_____
_____
_____
_____
_____

Live it Out *Practically*

Galatians 1:6

I am amazed that you are so quickly turning away from him who called you by the grace of Christ and are turning to a different gospel... (CSB)

APPLICATION QUESTIONS

For believers today to not turn to a different gospel, we need to practice spiritual scrutiny, paying close attention to what the true plan of salvation is.

- *We are not saved by following the law of Moses, we are saved by grace. (John 1:16-17)*
- *Second, we are not able to earn salvation through our actions or good works. It is a free gift from God. (Ephesians 2:8-9)*
- *Finally, what we need to do to be saved is respond to the gospel and place our faith in Jesus. (Romans 10:9-10)*

How would you use the above verses to explain in your own words the true gospel of Jesus Christ?

Where I *Saw* God today

Where I *Need* God today

Week 18

CHAPTER OF THE WEEK

Isaiah 6

HIGHLIGHTED VERSE

Isaiah 6:1

In the year that King Uzziah died, I saw the Lord, *high* and *exalted*, seated on a throne; and the train of his robe *filled the temple.*

Read it *Carefully*

Related *Verses*

Isaiah said this because he saw Jesus' glory and spoke about him.

JOHN 12:41

And the one who sat there had the appearance of jasper and ruby. A rainbow that shone like an emerald encircled the throne. Surrounding the throne were twenty-four other thrones, and seated on them were twenty-four elders. They were dressed in white and had crowns of gold on their heads. From the throne came flashes of lightning, rumblings and peals of thunder.

REVELATION 4:3-5

Your throne, O God, will last for ever and ever; a scepter of justice will be the scepter of your kingdom.

PSALM 45:6

Study it *Prayerfully*

IN ISAIAH 6, we get a glimpse of the throne room of God! King Uzziah had died and Isaiah entered the temple and he saw a very different king. He saw the King of Kings and the Lord of Lords on his throne high and lifted up and the train of his robe filled the temple.

The train of a gown or robe is that portion that hangs down in the back and sweeps across the floor. It signifies majesty and honor.

During Isaiah's time, the king's royal robe consisted of patches of the royal garments of kings that had fallen in defeat. The conquering king incorporated these pieces of cloth into his own robe as a symbol of the conqueror's strength and power. Isaiah looked at the train on God's robe and there were so many conquests until His robe "filled the temple" symbolizing that all of his enemies had been conquered.

No matter what happens in our world or who is ruling each nation, no matter if we are in a pandemic or war –Jesus is still on his throne. He is the King of kings and Lord of Lords. He sits on the throne of the universe and while other rulers live and die, He is alive forevermore and has defeated every enemy!

—Courtney

> *The Hebrew word for "Lord" is* **Adonai** *(pronounced ado-na-i). Adonai means Lord Master and is derived from the root word for sovereign one.*

MY **PRAYER** TO **GOD**

Creator God, help me to remember that You are sovereign over everything, even over . . .

_____
_____
_____
_____
_____
_____
_____

Live it Out *Practically*

Isaiah 6:1

In the year that King Uzziah died, I saw the Lord, high and exalted, seated on a throne; and the train of his robe filled the temple.

APPLICATION QUESTIONS

Do you struggle with fear when you watch the news? What current news story has you the most concerned or even fearful?

As we experience the rise and fall of presidents and of nations, how does it comfort you to remember that the King of kings and Lord of Lords is with you and he loves you?

Where I *Saw* God today

Where I *Need* God today

Week 19

CHAPTER OF THE WEEK

Galatians 1

HIGHLIGHTED VERSE

Galatians 1:10

Am I now trying to win the *approval* of human beings, or of God? Or am I trying to *please people*? If I were still trying to please people, I would not be a *servant of Christ*.

Read it *Carefully*

Related *Verses*

The fear of mankind is a snare, but the one who trusts in the Lord is protected.

PROVERBS 29:25 (CSB)

For they loved human praise more than praise from God.

JOHN 12:43 (CSB)

Peter and the apostles replied, "We must obey God rather than people.

ACTS 5:29 (CSB)

For we speak as messengers approved by God to be entrusted with the Good News. Our purpose is to please God, not people. He alone examines the motives of our hearts.

1 THESSALONIANS 2:4 (NLT)

Study it *Prayerfully*

IN GALATIANS 1:10, the Apostle Paul poses an important question, that's still relevant for us today: "Am I now trying to win the approval of human beings, or of God? Or am I trying to please people? If I were still trying to please people, I would not be a servant of Christ."

Hold up! Wait—what?! People in Bible times struggled with people-pleasing? Yes, they did.

The truth is there are so many times I give myself up to someone else's will rather than boldly and bravely choose to do what would most please God. When this happens, we are putting people in the place of God. This is an extremely dangerous practice.

However, God is able to help us break this pattern of people-pleasing. When we feel that twinge of tension, we can choose to prioritize pleasing God above placating people. We can determine to daringly speak the truth while being careful to avoid hurting someone's feelings.

Let's commit to seeking the Lord's plan rather than pursuing the approval of others. It won't always be easy, but God is continually faithful. He can teach us how to confidently live our lives despite the expectations and opinions of others.

—*Karen*

> *The Greek word for "please" in Galatians 1:10 is transliterated to English as* **aresko** *(pronounced ar-es'-ko). At its core, it means "to agree to satisfy another in order to win their approval, affection, or attention; to meet their expectations; to willingly serve."*

MY PRAYER TO GOD

Heavenly Father, I feel the tug of people pleasing when it comes to . . .

_____
_____
_____
_____
_____
_____
_____

Live it Out *Practically*

Galatians 1:10

Am I now trying to win the approval of human beings, or of God? Or am I trying to please people? If I were still trying to please people, I would not be a servant of Christ.

APPLICATION QUESTIONS

Proverbs 29:25 states that the fear of man is a snare or a trap. Have you ever felt trapped by your words or actions because you wanted the approval or admiration of someone else? What happened?

How might Paul's words in Galatians 1:10 give you the courage to not give in to people pleasing in the future?

Ponder this insightful–and true–phrase: "I do not need that person's permission to do God's will." Is there a situation in your life where you need to apply this phrase?

Where I *Saw* God today

Where I *Need* God today

Week 20

CHAPTER OF THE WEEK

Mark 8

HIGHLIGHTED VERSE

Mark 8:34

Then he called the *crowd* to him along with his *disciples* and said: "Whoever wants to be my disciple must *deny themselves* and take up their *cross* and *follow me.*"

Read it *Carefully*

Related *Verses*

"Whoever acknowledges me before others, I will also acknowledge before my Father in heaven. But whoever disowns me before others, I will disown before my Father in heaven."

MATTHEW 10:32-33

Therefore, I urge you, brothers and sisters, in view of God's mercy, to offer your bodies as a living sacrifice, holy and pleasing to God—this is your true and proper worship. Do not conform to the pattern of this world, but be transformed by the renewing of your mind. Then you will be able to test and approve what God's will is—his good, pleasing and perfect will.

ROMANS 12:1-2

I have been crucified with Christ and I no longer live, but Christ lives in me. The life I now live in the body, I live by faith in the Son of God, who loved me and gave himself for me.

GALATIANS 2:20

Study it *Prayerfully*

JESUS SAYS ANYONE CAN FOLLOW HIM. Anyone who is young, old, male, female, no matter what sins we have committed—anyone and everyone is invited to follow Jesus. Choosing to follow him means that he is at the lead. We come after him. We can't choose our own path or go our own way. We walk behind him and as we walk behind him, we say no to ourselves.

Many follow Jesus right up until it gets hard and then fall away. Jesus does not promise a comfy, cozy, perfect life. If anyone comes after Jesus, it's a denial of self and a commitment fully to him. He promises a cross to his followers where we come and die to ourselves and find life in him.

Will you choose to follow Jesus, even when the way gets rocky? God never promised that our lives would be easy. He did, however, promise to never leave us or forsake us as we follow him in this life. (Hebrews 13:5)

—*Courtney*

> *The Greek word for "deny" is* **aparneomai** *(pronounced ap-ar-neh'-om-ahee). Aparneomai means to utterly deny, abstain from or completely disown.*

MY **PRAYER** TO **GOD**

Jesus, even when life gets hard, I want to follow close behind You. Enable me to . . .

_____
_____
_____
_____
_____
_____
_____
_____

Live it Out *Practically*

Mark 8:34

Then he called the crowd to him along with his disciples and said: "Whoever wants to be my disciple must deny themselves and take up their cross and follow me."

APPLICATION QUESTIONS

Who or what are you following in your life today? List anything here that comes to your mind that is NOT God.

Now, what adjustments in your life might you need to make so you can more closely follow after God? Be specific. In the end, the answer to this question will be the only thing that matters.

Where I *Saw* God today

Where I *Need* God today

Week 21

CHAPTER OF THE WEEK

Proverbs 18

HIGHLIGHTED VERSE

Proverbs 18:21

Death and *life* are in the *power* of the *tongue* and those who love it will *eat its fruit.* (CSB)

Read it *Carefully*

Related *Verses*

Every kind of animal, bird, reptile, and fish is tamed and has been tamed by humankind, but no one can tame the tongue. It is a restless evil, full of deadly poison.

JAMES 3:7-8 (CSB)

No foul language should come from your mouth, but only what is good for building up someone in need, so that it gives grace to those who hear.

EPHESIANS 4:29 (CSB)

A gentle answer turns away anger, but a harsh word stirs up wrath. The tongue of the wise makes knowledge attractive, but the mouth of fools blurts out foolishness.

PROVERBS 15:1-2 (CSB)

Study it *Prayerfully*

"DEATH AND LIFE ARE IN THE POWER OF THE TONGUE . . . " warns Proverbs 18:21. Have you ever been on the receiving end of life-giving words? Then, at other times, has something cruel or unkind been spoken to you, where the words lodged in your brain, bringing you sorrow each time you recalled them?

This very day, you will have many opportunities to use your words. In our interactions with the people who cross our paths—family, friends, co-workers or complete strangers—we can utter words that instill hope, wholeness and courage to others. Or our statements can kill—dashing dreams, crushing confidence and dragging someone's spirit down.

Whether we are speaking face-to-face, talking on the phone or even using our digital tongues in a comment thread or text message, remember this: Our words are powerful, and they have consequences. Will your words be a weapon of demolition or a wonderful tool that creates something of beauty?

May we be ever mindful of the way our words might impact those to whom we speak. Let's aspire to use our speech with godly purpose.

To build . . . not to break. To bless . . . not to badger. To praise . . . not to pounce.

—*Karen*

> *The Hebrew word for our English phrase "in the power" in Proverbs 18:21 is* **yad** *(pronounced* yawd*) and its definition is strength and power held in your two hands. It can also mean a weapon in the hands.*

MY PRAYER TO GOD

Lord God, I want my words today to . . .

___
___
___
___
___
___
___

Live it Out *Practically*

Proverbs 18:21

Death and life are in the power of the tongue and those who love it will eat its fruit. (CSB)

APPLICATION **QUESTIONS**

Do you have any phrases from the past ricocheting in your mind or embedded in your heart? Were they uplifting or demoralizing? Words of life, or remarks of death?

Let the fact that you can still recall these words be a powerful reminder to carefully and prayerfully speak to others this week. What is one way you can use your words today to bring life rather than to deal a death blow?

Where I *Saw* God today

Where I *Need* God today

Week 22

CHAPTER OF THE WEEK

Psalm 42

HIGHLIGHTED VERSE

Psalm 42:1

As the *deer* pants for streams of *water*, so my *soul* pants for you, my *God*.

Read it *Carefully*

Related *Verses*

You, God, are my God, earnestly I seek you; I thirst for you, my whole being longs for you, in a dry and parched land where there is no water.

PSALM 63:

My soul yearns for you in the night; in the morning my spirit longs for you.

ISAIAH 26:

And without faith it is impossible to please God, because anyone who comes to him must believe that he exists and that he rewards those who earnestly seek him.

HEBREWS 11:

Study it *Prayerfully*

WHAT IS YOUR SOUL LONGING FOR TODAY? Are you going through life panting—trying to find streams that will quench your thirst but ending up unsatisfied and at a dead-end road?

So many times, we are tempted to try to fix our souls by doing external things like eating, shopping, scrolling on social media, talking with friends, going on vacation, getting a new hair color or lipstick shade. None of this helps our soul. Instead, it can waste our time and divert our attention away from what matters most: our relationship with Jesus.

Our souls were made to find rest in God alone. We were made to know and walk with God. Everything that happens externally of us is temporary, but our soul is eternal. Your soul is the most important part of you! I often say, the ultimate self-care is soul care. Tend to your soul today by spending time with the Lord.

—*Courtney*

> *In Psalm 42:1, the Hebrew word for "pant" is* **arag** *(pronounced aw-rag'). Arag means to long for, to pant, or to cry out.*

MY PRAYER TO GOD

Father, I want to long for You more than anyone or anything. Please help me to . . .

Live it Out *Practically*

Psalm 42:1

As the deer pants for streams of water, so my soul pants for you, my God.

APPLICATION QUESTIONS

What are some common things that we are tempted to long for in our current culture? List all you can think of.

Take an inventory of your thoughts and your actions and then answer this question: Do you long for the Lord or do you tend to long for things of this world? How do you want this to change?

Where I *Saw* God today

Where I *Need* God today

Week 23

CHAPTER OF THE WEEK

Hosea 12

HIGHLIGHTED VERSE

Hosea 12:6

But you must *return* to your God. Maintain *love* and *justice*, and always put your *hope* in God. (CSB)

Read it *Carefully*

Related *Verses*

All a person's ways seem right to him, but the Lord weighs hearts.

PROVERBS 21:2 (CSB)

The counsel of the Lord stands forever, the plans of his heart from generation to generation.

PSALM 33:1

We all went astray like sheep; we all have turned to our own way; and the Lord has punished him for the iniquity of us all.

ISAIAH 53:6 (CSB)

Study it *Prayerfully*

SOMETIMES I WONDER what we look like to God when we try to get our own way. We plot. We plan. We try to get others on our side as we attempt to sway opinions and fix outcomes. And we aren't the first ones to do it.

In the Old Testament book of Hosea, we see Israel trying to befriend and appease the superpowers of the time that would bring their nation peace and prosperity. They depended on these schemes rather than depending on the Lord. However, the idols Israel worshiped and the alliances they made with foreigners would leave the nation dry and even destroyed.

Then, in Hosea 12:6, the people are told to come back to God, act with love, pursue justice and depend solely upon Him. He is the God who rescues and warns and if the people will listen to Hosea and submit to God's commands, they will be brought back into a right relationship with the Lord.

How often we too try to plan out our own way, not realizing the danger that lies in approaching life this way. May we instead pursue God's ways and his will, saving ourselves a boatload of regret and sorrow.

—*Karen*

> *The Hebrew word for "hope" in Hosea 12:6 is the phrase* **qavah** *(pronounced kaw-vaw') and it literally means to twist and stretch in a tension of enduring and waiting upon.*

MY PRAYER TO GOD

Powerful God, I don't want to take matters into my own hands. I want to hope in You when it comes to . . .

_____
_____
_____
_____
_____
_____
_____

Live it Out *Practically*

Hosea 12:6

But you must return to your God. Maintain love and justice, and always put your hope in God. (CSB)

APPLICATION QUESTIONS

When we too wrestle with God today, trying to get situations to go our way, we can keep in mind the following:

1. God's grace extends to everyone, even rogues and exiles.
We must never for a moment think that God's grace is only for the good. Hosea shows us that God's love was available for unfaithful Israel. Today, God's grace is still available when we are unfaithful too.

2. Our struggles should lead to surrender.
The Lord's dealing with his people in the time of Hosea shows us a God always willing to forgive and redeem. Surrender brings success. It is then that we are able to trade our brokenness for God's blessing.

Which of the above two statements do you most need to keep in mind today and why?

Where I *Saw* God today

Where I *Need* God today

Week 24

CHAPTER OF THE WEEK

Matthew 6

HIGHLIGHTED VERSE

Matthew 6:6

"But when you *pray*, go into your room, close the door and pray to your *Father*, who is unseen. Then your Father, who sees what is done in *secret*, will *reward* you."

Read it *Carefully*

Related *Verses*

And when you pray, do not be like the hypocrites, for they love to pray standing in the synagogues and on the street corners to be seen by others. Truly I tell you, they have received their reward in full.

MATTHEW 6:

And when you pray, do not keep on babbling like pagans, for they think they will be heard because of their many words. Do not be like them, for your Father knows what you need before you ask him.

MATTHEW 6:7-

Very early in the morning, while it was still dark, Jesus got up, left the house and went off to a solitary place, where he prayed.

MARK 1:3

Study it *Prayerfully*

JESUS SAID WHEN WE PRAY, we are not to pray with the goal of being seen and praised by others. God is not impressed when we pray eloquent prayers in public. This does not mean we should not pray in public but rather when we do pray in public, we must watch the motivation of our heart.

Jesus said it is the hidden prayers of his people that he rewards. Do you have a place where you get alone to pray? Maybe you have a chair in your family room, or you prefer your kitchen table? Perhaps it's inside your car or a bench at the park. In my college dorm, I would go to the stairwell or shower stall to get alone to pray and when my kids were little, I used the bathroom!

It is not as much about the place as it is about the prayer. There is power in our hidden prayers to the Lord. So, pick a place and set a time. Then, show up and meet with the Lord through the wonderful communication tool of prayer!

—*Courtney*

> *The Greek word for "secret" in Matthew 6:6 is the word **kruptos** (pronounced kroop-tos'). Kruptos means to be private, concealed, or to hide away from.*

MY **PRAYER** TO **GOD**

Lord God, I long to meet with You in the secret places in my heart. Today I will . . .

_____
_____
_____
_____
_____
_____
_____

Live it Out *Practically*

Matthew 6:6

"But when you pray, go into your room, close the door and pray to your Father, who is unseen. Then your Father, who sees what is done in secret, will reward you."

APPLICATION QUESTIONS

Where are your favorite places to get alone with the Lord and pray? List any you can think of from the past here below.

If you do not have a special meeting place to pray, choose one today and begin a habit of going there daily to meet with God. Where will this place be and when will you meet with God there next?

Where I *Saw* God today

Where I *Need* God today

Week 25

CHAPTER OF THE WEEK

Jonah 1

HIGHLIGHTED VERSE

Jonah 1:5

The sailors were *afraid,*
and each *cried* out to his god... (CSB)

Read it *Carefully*

Related *Verses*

In my desperation I prayed, and the LORD listened; he saved me from all my troubles.

PSALM 34:6 (NLT)

I call to you from the ends of the earth when my heart is without strength. Lead me to a rock that is high above me,...

PSALM 61:2 (CSB)

I cry aloud to God, aloud to God, and he will hear me. I sought the Lord in my day of trouble.

PSALM 77:1-2 (CSB)

Study it *Prayerfully*

A GROUP OF SEAFARERS had a scary trip on a ship headed from Joppa to Tarshish. On the vessel was a passenger, Jonah of Amittai. Yes, that Jonah—the one who wound up inside the big belly of a whale. Instead of obeying God when told to go to Nineveh to preach to the people there, Jonah turned on his heels and fled in the exact opposite direction, purchasing a ticket to Tarshish, a city in Spain, instead.

Once aboard the ship, the Lord caused a mighty storm that heaved the ship violently upon the crashing waves. This must have been a squall of great magnitude because we read that the hearty mariners, who were used to sailing in storms, became extremely afraid, each crying out to his god.

When the idols failed to answer, the seamen took matters into their own hands, chucking cargo overboard in order to lighten the ship. But neither the storm, nor their fears, subsided. The crew then cast lots to see which passenger on board had caused the storm. When the lot fell to Jonah, he fessed up about his runaway tale and urged them to promptly toss him overboard. Thus, his infamous ride in the belly of a whale.

It wasn't until the sailors obeyed God's servant Jonah's instructions that God finally calmed the seas. These rough and tumble men then stopped fearing the elements and began to fear God instead, the Creator of the wind and the waves.

—*Karen*

> *The name Jonah means dove in Hebrew and may indicate he had a tender spirit.* **Amittai** *is the Hebrew word for truth, which was appropriate for a prophet who was supposed to declare the word of the Lord.*

MY **PRAYER** TO **GOD**

Father, in the midst of the storm raging around me, empower me to . . .

_____
_____
_____
_____
_____
_____
_____

Live it Out *Practically*

Jonah 1:5

The sailors were afraid, and each cried out to his god. (CSB)

APPLICATION QUESTIONS

Is there a storm you are currently walking through in life? It may be physical, emotional, or spiritual. Name that storm here.

How might others in your life - who are in fear of their circumstances and futilely placing trust in false things - come to fear and revere God when they see you acting in obedience today, even in the midst of a storm?

Where I *Saw* God today

Where I *Need* God today

Week 26

CHAPTER OF THE WEEK

Proverbs 3

HIGHLIGHTED VERSES

Proverbs 3:5-6

Trust in the Lord with all your *heart* and lean not on your own *understanding*. In all your ways *submit* to him, and he will make your *paths straight*.

Read it *Carefully*

Related *Verses*

Those who know your name trust in you, for you, Lord, have never forsaken those who seek you.

PSALM 9:1

Some trust in chariots and some in horses, but we trust in the name of the Lord our God.

PSALM 20:

And we know that in all things God works for the good of those who love him, who have been called according to his purpose.

ROMANS 8:2

Study it *Prayerfully*

GOD TELLS US TO TRUST IN HIM with all of our heart. Not part of our heart. Not even half of our heart. This means we are to have full confidence in him and rely on him and his wisdom rather than trusting in ourselves and our own knowledge. He says that when we follow his ways, he will guide us. He will give us the wisdom we need to direct our paths.

In Bible times, horses and chariots struck fear in the hearts of the military men. They symbolized strength. But David said, he would not trust in his horses and chariots because they could not compare with the strength of the Lord our God. I don't know what troubles you are facing today but I pray that this would be said of us -- that in the midst of our difficult times, we trust in the name of the Lord our God.

—*Courtney*

> *The Hebrew word for "trust" in Proverbs 3:5-6 is* **batach** *(pronounced baw-takh'). Batach means to trust, to be confident and certain, or to be sure of or to put your hope in.*

MY **PRAYER** TO GOD

Dear Lord, I want to trust in You with all of my heart, not just part of it. Today I will . . .

_____
_____
_____
_____
_____
_____
_____

Live it Out *Practically*

Proverbs 3:5-6

Trust in the Lord with all your heart and lean not on your own understanding. In all your ways submit to him, and he will make your paths straight.

APPLICATION QUESTIONS

If you were to look at how you spend your time and what (or who) you think about, what conclusions could you draw about who or what you are trusting in most to-day? Is it your own strength, your bank account, your spouse, a friend, or anything else this world offers?

Now, what might you need to start doing differently to trust in God more than you trust in other people or things?

Determine today to put all of your trust in God alone.

Where I *Saw* God today

Where I *Need* God today

Week 27

CHAPTER OF THE WEEK

Amos 7

HIGHLIGHTED VERSE

Amos 7:7

He *showed* me this: The Lord was *standing* there by a vertical wall with a *plumb line* in his *hand*. (CSB)

Read it *Carefully*

Related *Verses*

The one who has my commands and keeps them is the one who loves me. And the one who loves me will be loved by my Father. I also will love him and will reveal myself to him.

JOHN 14:21 (CSB)

This is love: that we walk according to his commands. This is the command as you have heard it from the beginning: that you walk in love.

2 JOHN 1:6 (CSB)

Go, therefore, and make disciples of all nations, baptizing them in the name of the Father and of the Son and of the Holy Spirit, teaching them to observe everything I have commanded you. And remember, I am with you always, to the end of the age.

MATTHEW 28:19-20 (CSB)

Study it *Prayerfully*

ONE DAY, THE OLD TESTAMENT PROPHET AMOS sees three visions. One of these is that of a plumb line. This tool involves a cord with a weight at one end that is held up to the top of a structure. As gravity pulls the weight downward, you can determine whether vertical structures are straight by comparison.

Here, the image of a plumb line is used symbolically to refer to the godly standard against which the Lord would measure the behavior of his people. He had found Israel's leadership to be chronically crooked, and as a result, the nation would be judged harshly, being laid waste as the house of Jeroboam fell by the sword.

We can glean a few concepts for our lives and behavior from this vivid account of the three visions.

God has standards. God hasn't left us to fend for ourselves, trying to figure out how to live our lives here on earth. His Word is our plumb line, and in Scripture we find both directives for living as well as warnings for what might happen when we ignore his instructions.

Each of us has a response to his standards. We have a choice. We can choose to follow after God, obeying his commands, or we can reject his standards and make up our own rules in life. Each choice has ramifications.

Praise God for both his plumb line, which shows us how to live, and his mercy shown to us when our behavior fails to measure up to his standards.

—*Karen*

> *There is more than one Hebrew word for God in the Old Testament. The Hebrew word for Lord in Amos 7:7 is* **Adonay** *(pronounced* ad-o-noy'*) and is used as a proper name of God only. It also doesn't just mean the Lord in general, by it means personally my Lord.*

MY **PRAYER** TO **GOD**

My Lord, may Your Word be a plumb line in my life when it comes to . . .

_____
_____
_____
_____
_____
_____
_____

Live it Out *Practically*

Amos 7:7

He showed me this: The Lord was standing there by a vertical wall with a plumb line in his hand. (CSB)

APPLICATION QUESTIONS

Even when we choose wrongly, the Lord's mercy triumphs over His judgment. Just as with Amos, God is ready to grant mercy when we humbly ask for it. His primary motive is mercy. And his ultimate act of mercy was in sending Jesus, his only Son and the one true prophet, to offer us forgiveness and save us.

Is there an area in your current life where you need the Lord's mercy? What will you ask him to do for you in this situation?

Where I *Saw* God today

Where I *Need* God today

Week 28

CHAPTER OF THE WEEK

Romans 4

HIGHLIGHTED VERSE

Romans 4:18

Against all *hope*, Abraham in hope *believed* and so became the *father* of many nations.

Read it *Carefully*

Related *Verses*

And without faith it is impossible to please God, because anyone who comes to him must believe that he exists and that he rewards those who earnestly seek him.

HEBREWS 11:

He replied, "Because you have so little faith. Truly I tell you, if you have faith as small as a mustard seed, you can say to this mountain, 'Move from here to there,' and it will move. Nothing will be impossible for you."

MATTHEW 17:2

Study it *Prayerfully*

WE TALK A LOT ABOUT HAVING STRONGER FAITH, and many people even encourage one another with the familiar phrase, "have faith." But what does that really look like? It is one thing to try to have faith, it is quite another to walk in faith. Walking by faith requires action and risk. We put what we believe on the line and live it out.

The story of Abraham in the Bible is a perfect example of this. Abraham left everything to go where God was calling him, and he faced many challenges. Romans 4:18 says, "Against all hope," which tells us that this wasn't easy for Abraham. But guess what? Verse 18 goes on to say, "Abraham believed."

So, even in the face of challenges and resistance and seemingly impossible circumstances, Abraham walked by faith. He believed. God wants us to have the same faith that follows him where he leads. Our obedience is the place where God shows up and does his greatest work in and through us.

—*Ruth*

> *Faith or belief is a gift from God. To "believe," in Romans 4:18 is the Greek word* **pisteuó** *(pronounced pist-yoo'-o), is to commit oneself in complete and absolute trust. It is faith in God, but also faithfulness to God.*

MY **PRAYER** TO **GOD**

Gracious Lord, I need to believe You against all hope when it comes to . . .

_____
_____
_____
_____
_____
_____
_____
_____

Live it Out *Practically*

Romans 4:18

Against all hope, Abraham in hope believed and so became the father of many nations.

APPLICATION QUESTIONS

What stops you from walking in faith? List any things you can think of here.

How does the phrase "against all hope' encourage or inspire you?

What is God calling you to do that you have been pushing aside out of fear? How will you approach this situation differently in the future?

Where I *Saw* God today

Where I *Need* God today

Week 29

CHAPTER OF THE WEEK

Romans 5

HIGHLIGHTED VERSES

Romans 5:6-8

You see, at just the right *time*, when we were still *powerless*, Christ died for the ungodly. Very rarely will anyone die for a *righteous person*, though for a good person someone might possibly dare to die. But God demonstrates his own *love* for us in this: While we were still sinners, *Christ died for us.*

Read it *Carefully*

Related *Verses*

For God so loved the world that he gave his one and only Son, that whoever believes in him shall not perish but have eternal life.

JOHN 3:1

My command is this: Love each other as I have loved you. Greater love has no one than this: to lay down one's life for one's friends.

JOHN 15:12-1

And I pray that you, being rooted and established in love, may have power, together with all the Lord's holy people, to grasp how wide and long and high and deep is the love of Christ, and to know this love that surpasses knowledge—that you may be filled to the measure of all the fullness of God.

EPHESIANS 3:17-1

Study it *Prayerfully*

THERE IS NO GREATER PROOF or evidence of God's love for us, than Jesus' death on the cross. While we were ungodly sinners and powerless to save ourselves, Christ went first. He died for us and now we are reconciled to him and we get to experience the abundance of his love, poured out on us daily.

When God saved us from our sins, we escaped his coming wrath, but we did not get to escape all the hardships that come along with this life. Instead, we get to live our lives with the presence of a loving Heavenly Father, who is always with us. He goes before us and guides, comforts, strengthens, and protects us. Look for the hand of God on your hard days, ordinary days, and happy days.

You are loved! Rest in that love today.

—*Courtney*

> *The Greek word in Romans 5:6-8 for "demonstrates" is* **sunistanó** *(pronounced soon-is-tah'-o) which means to exhibit or introduce; to establish or stand near.*

MY **PRAYER** TO **GOD**

Dear God, as I think about all You have done for me, I thank You for . . .

_____
_____
_____
_____
_____
_____
_____

Live it Out *Practically*

Romans 5:6-8

You see, at just the right time, when we were still powerless, Christ died for the ungodly. Very rarely will anyone die for a righteous person, though for a good person someone might possibly dare to die. But God demonstrates his own love for us in this: While we were still sinners, Christ died for us.

APPLICATION QUESTIONS

How does remembering Christ's death on the cross for you make you feel? List all the feelings you can think of such as loved, cherished, wanted, etc...

How have you experienced the continued love of God in your life, this week? List specific ways below.

Where I *Saw* God today

Where I *Need* God today

Week 30

CHAPTER OF THE WEEK

Judges 15

HIGHLIGHTED VERSE

Judges 15:15

He found a fresh jawbone of a *donkey*, *reached* out his hand, took it, and *killed* a thousand men with it. (CSB)

Read it *Carefully*

Related *Verses*

For this is what love for God is: to keep his commands. And his commands are not a burden, because everyone who has been born of God conquers the world. This is the victory that has conquered the world: our faith.

1 JOHN 5:3-4 (CSB)

For the Lord your God is the one who goes with you to fight for you against your enemies to give you victory.

DEUTERONOMY 20:4 (CSB)

In conclusion, be strong in the Lord [draw your strength from Him and be empowered through your union with Him] and in the power of His [boundless] might.

EPHESIANS 6:10 (AMP)

Study it *Prayerfully*

I AM ALWAYS FASCINATED by the way God takes something ordinary, combines it with a little faith and obedience from His followers, and then uses it to display His glory and show forth His power.

In the book of Judges, we encounter Samson, who one day wielded a simple object—the jawbone of a donkey—that God provided as a rather unconventional weapon. That improvised instrument, powered by the Spirit of the Lord, enabled Samson to strike down 1,000 Philistines.

In his encounter with his enemies, Samson was not alone. The Spirit of the Lord was powerfully on him. This wasn't the first time God's Spirit gave Samson victory. The Spirit was also with him when he tore a lion apart with his bare hands and when he struck down 30 men of Ashkelon in Judges 14.

Today, when we are facing spiritual battles, the victory is ours through our Lord Jesus Christ. He will never leave us or abandon us. (Hebrews 13:5) He will be with us to the end of the age. (Matthew 28:20) The Spirit of the Lord momentarily came upon Samson to empower him, and the Holy Spirit always helps us as believers today, guides us in all truth, and is our ever-present defender whenever we face a spiritual battle. (John 14:26-27; 16:13)

—*Karen*

> *The Hebrew word for "took" in Judges 15:15 is* **laqach** *(pronounced* plaw-kakh'*) and it means to take possession of; to accept and carry along with oneself.*

MY **PRAYER** TO **GOD**

Father, although I feel ordinary, I know You can grant me victory in . . .

_____
_____
_____
_____
_____
_____
_____

Live it Out *Practically*

Judges 15:15

He found a fresh jawbone of a donkey, reached out his hand, took it, and killed a thousand men with it. (CSB)

APPLICATION QUESTIONS

The same God who empowered Samson through his spirit is available to us today when we face our battles in life. How does acknowledging—and then relying on—the fact that the Holy Spirit dwells in you today make it easier for you to walk through life's storms or make important decisions?

What is one action step you will take this week as you face a decision or battle through a storm? Write it out in the space provided.

Where I *Saw* God today

Where I *Need* God today

Week 31

CHAPTER OF THE WEEK

Ephesians 5

HIGHLIGHTED VERSE

Ephesians 5:15

Be very *careful*, then, how you *live*—
not as *unwise*, but as *wise*.

Read it *Carefully*

Related *Verses*

Jesus answered, "I am the way and the truth and the life. No one comes to the Father except through me."

JOHN 14:

Folly brings joy to one who has no sense, but whoever has understanding keeps a straight course.

PROVERBS 15:2

"I am sending you out like sheep among wolves. Therefore be as shrewd as snakes and as innocent as doves..."

MATTHEW 10:1

Study it *Prayerfully*

MOST THINGS IN LIFE we want to learn take study and practice. Everything from cooking to running to singing and so on. It takes intentional practice to become skilled at something. The same goes for life with God.

In the Old Testament, the word wisdom in Hebrew doesn't just mean intelligence or some sort of super-spiritual knowing; it is often translated in the Bible as "skilled." In our verse in the New Testament, Ephesians 5:15, we are instructed to "be wise," or we might say, we need to be very careful to live a skilled life.

Skill takes practice and time. We aren't born living by God's standards. It is something we learn over time when we go to his Word and spend time with him in prayer. There is a wise way and a foolish way to walk through life.

As followers of Jesus, we are commanded to be wise, or skilled, in how we live. This means everything from skill in parenting to skill in our thoughts or how we use our time. We can't just hope for the best, we must work at it, with God's help. The good news is that we have the perfect example to follow. His name is Jesus.

—*Ruth*

> *The Greek word for "wise" is* **sophos** *(pronounced* sof-os*). It means learned or diligent. This is precise and intentional living.*

MY **PRAYER** TO **GOD**

Heavenly Father, I need You to empower me to be skilled and wise about...

_____
_____
_____
_____
_____
_____
_____

Live it Out *Practically*

Ephesians 5:15

Be very careful, then, how you live–not as unwise, but as wise.

APPLICATION QUESTIONS

Are there areas of your life where you need to become more skilled? List any you can think of here.

How can you learn from Jesus' example? What is one action step you can take this week to show wisdom and skill in your life?

Where I *Saw* God today

Where I *Need* God today

Week 32

CHAPTER OF THE WEEK

1 Thessalonians 5

HIGHLIGHTED VERSES

1 Thessalonians 5:16-18

Rejoice always, pray continually, give thanks in all circumstances; for this is God's will for you in Christ Jesus.

Read it Carefully

Related Verses

Enter his gates with thanksgiving and his courts with praise; give thanks to him and praise his name.

PSALM 100:

Give thanks to the Lord, for he is good. His love endures forever.

PSALM 136

Let the peace of Christ rule in your hearts, since as members of one body you were called to peace. And be thankful.

COLOSSIANS 3:1

Study it *Prayerfully*

GOD KNOWS WHAT THE HUMAN HEART NEEDS and it needs to rejoice always, pray continually, and give thanks. This is God's good will for us. Giving thanks takes our focus off the things that we are worried about and puts our focus on the good things in life.

What we focus on grows. That is why giving thanks is an important spiritual discipline. It helps open our eyes to the good gifts that God has generously given to us each day. Interestingly, it is also scientifically proven that listing the things we are grateful for improves our relationships, our mood, our sleep, our hopefulness, our resiliency and our physical and psychological health.

Let's grow our thankfulness to the Lord this week. So many times we wonder what God's will is for our lives – this is God's will for you!

—*Courtney*

> *The Greek word for "thanks" in 1 Thessalonians 5:16-18 is **eucharisteo** (pronounced yoo-khar-is-teh'-o). Eucharisteo means to be grateful or to give thanks as an act of spiritual worship to God.*

MY **PRAYER** TO GOD

Father, Your word says to give thanks in all circumstances. So, I am giving You thanks today even though . . .

_____
_____
_____
_____
_____
_____
_____

Live it Out *Practically*

1 Thessalonians 5:16-18

Rejoice always, pray continually, give thanks in all circumstances; for this is God's will for you in Christ Jesus.

APPLICATION QUESTIONS

If we are to give thanks in all circumstances, then there isn't a single situation in our lives for which we should be ungrateful. Pause right now and list 5 things, situations, or people for which you are grateful, even if some of them are not so pleasant. (Remember, ALL circumstances!)

Now, pause right now to pray and give thanks to God for each one of these five things or situations.

Where I *Saw* God today

Where I *Need* God today

Week 33

CHAPTER OF THE WEEK

1 Kings 3

HIGHLIGHTED VERSE

1 Kings 3:9

So give your *servant* a discerning *heart* to *govern* your people and to distinguish between *right* and *wrong*. For who is able to govern this great people of yours?

Read it *Carefully*

Related *Verses*

Guard your heart above all else, for it is the source of life.

PROVERBS 4:23 (CSB)

As water reflects the face, so the heart reflects the person.

PROVERBS 27:19 (CSB)

A good person produces good out of the good stored up in his heart. An evil person produces evil out of the evil stored up in his heart, for his mouth speaks from the overflow of the heart.

LUKE 6:45 (CSB)

Study it *Prayerfully*

IT IS DURING A UNIQUE COMMUNICATION SESSION between Solomon and God in 1 Kings 3 that God utters a stunning statement, "Ask for whatever you want me to give you" Wow! What an open door! This wasn't some fictitious genie in a bottle. This was Almighty God presenting Solomon with this incredible offer.

Solomon still doesn't jump directly to his request. He gives credit to God for his position as king. Then finally, a full six sentences into his reply, Solomon makes his request known. What did he want? Incredible military success? Adoring loyalty of the people in his kingdom? A long and healthy life? Nope. None of these things. Solomon humbly requests a discerning heart.

His answer pleased the Lord greatly. And so, God not only granted Solomon what he asked for, but he also gifted him with blessings he didn't request: wealth, honor and—if he would walk in obedience to God—a long life.

—*Karen*

> *The Hebrew word for "discerning" is **bin** (pronounced bene) and it means a careful pondering or investigative scrutinizing or a clever consideration.*

MY **PRAYER** TO **GOD**

Father, please give me a discerning heart in the area of . . .

_____
_____
_____
_____
_____
_____
_____

Live it Out *Practically*

1 Kings 3:9

So give your servant a discerning heart to govern your people and to distinguish between right and wrong. For who is able to govern this great people of yours?

APPLICATION **QUESTIONS**

Do you long for a heart of discernment? May Solomon's humble interaction with God serve as an example for all of us as we make our appeals to Him and as we use the gift he has granted us to humbly and rightly serve others. Here are three principles to remember:

1. Start with God's character before you give your requests.
2. Know your place– God is God, and you are not.
3. Use the answers to your prayers to serve others.

Which of these three principles most speaks to you today and why?

Where I *Saw* God today

Where I *Need* God today

Week 34

CHAPTER OF THE WEEK

Genesis 16

HIGHLIGHTED VERSE

Genesis 16:13

"You are the *God* who *sees* me."

Read it *Carefully*

Related *Verses*

In a desert land he found him, in a barren and howling waste. He shielded him and cared for him; he guarded him as the apple of his eye,...

DEUTERONOMY 32:1

The Lord will keep you from all harm— he will watch over your life; the Lord will watch over your coming and going both now and forevermore.

PSALM 121:7-

I am with you and will watch over you wherever you go, and I will bring you back to this land. I will not leave you until I have done what I have promised you."

GENESIS 28:1

Study it *Prayerfully*

HAVE YOU FOUND YOURSELF IN A DESERT feeling thirsty and wondering why God hasn't shown up? You are in good company because the Old Testament character Hagar felt the same way.

Hagar isn't typically mentioned as one of the heroes of the faith but rather a scandalous side note in the story of Abraham and Sarah's pursuit to have a child. After many years of waiting, they took matters into their own hands, and the maidservant of Sarah, Hagar was offered to Abraham to have their child. However, when Hagar was found to be pregnant, Sarah became jealous and began to mistreat her, so she was forced to flee her camp.

Genesis 16:13 picks up with Hagar alone and helpless and hiding near a spring in the desert. I love Hagar's response to God finding her: "You are the God who sees me." Hagar is the first person in the Bible to use "another name" for God. In particular, she uses the name (in Hebrew) El Roi. The name literally means the God who sees me.

Though Hagar and her unborn child were out of sight and out of mind, the eyes of the LORD were upon her. Hagar gives us an important truth about our own visibility under the gaze of a loving God who sees beyond what others cannot. No matter how lonely and desperate our situation is, God sees us right where we are, and He won't leave us.

—Ruth

> *In Hebrew, "**El-Roi**," means God (**El**) sees me (**Roi**). It is pronounced ēl-rŏ-î. We are never truly out of God's sight.*

MY **PRAYER** TO **GOD**

Dear Lord, I need to know that You see me when I think about . . .

Live it Out *Practically*

Genesis 16:13
You are the God who sees me.

APPLICATION QUESTIONS

Is there an area of your life where God seems absent? Briefly describe that situation here.

How does the story of Hagar encourage you to turn to God, the one who sees you?

Where I *Saw* God today

Where I *Need* God today

Week 35

CHAPTER OF THE WEEK

John 6

HIGHLIGHTED VERSE

John 6:35

Jesus declared, "I am the *bread of life*. Whoever *comes* to me will never go hungry, and whoever *believes* in me will never be *thirsty*."

Read it *Carefully*

Related *Verses*

When Jesus spoke again to the people, he said, "I am the light of the world. Whoever follows me will never walk in darkness, but will have the light of life."

JOHN 8:1

His divine power has given us everything we need for a godly life through our knowledge of him who called us by his own glory and goodness.

2 PETER 1:

"I am the true vine, and my Father is the gardener."

JOHN 15

Study it *Prayerfully*

I AM A SELF-PROCLAIMED FOODIE. I love farm-to-table restaurants and even have a mental list of all my very favorite meals from different restaurants across the country. I've even been known to get very animated while eating. Ha! There is just something so satisfying about the taste of really good food. But no matter how amazing a meal that I eat is, I am still left empty because, yes, food fills my stomach temporarily. It isn't long and I am hungry again. I need more. Something deeper.

That is why Jesus' declaration shortly after feeding the five thousand with manna means so much. It didn't take long, and the crowds were looking for more food to eat! We are all "hungry." We do our best to fill that deep soul hunger with lots of stuff, whether it is new clothes, looking a certain way, or that next job promotion. But our true source of strength and happiness isn't from anything we get or do, it is from Jesus. He tells us we can come to Him for true and lasting satisfaction. Nothing else will do.

Jesus is the real bread, the Bread of Life. Our sustenance can only be found in him. We, too, must learn that while manna temporarily satisfies, only Jesus satisfies our spiritual needs forever.

—*Ruth*

> *To be "hungry," or* **peinao** *(pronounced* pi-nah'-o*) in Greek, denotes to be needy. This isn't just a physical need. This is an earnest desire for something more. A deep spiritual need that can only be satisfied in Jesus.*

MY **PRAYER** TO **GOD**

Jesus, it is only You who truly satisfies. Help me to hunger for . . .

_____
_____
_____
_____
_____
_____
_____

Live it Out *Practically*

John 6:35

Jesus declared, "I am the bread of life. Whoever comes to me will never go hungry, and whoever believes in me will never be thirsty."

APPLICATION **QUESTIONS**

What does our culture hunger after? Name any things, positions, or situations you can think of.

What would it look like for you to find your hunger satisfied completely in Jesus? How would things change for you?

What is one change you will make in your life to hunger after Jesus rather than after what the world offers.

Where I *Saw* God today

Where I *Need* God today

Week 36

CHAPTER OF THE WEEK

Psalm 121

HIGHLIGHTED VERSES

Psalm 121:1-2

I lift up my *eyes* to the *mountains*—
where does my *help* come from?
My help comes from the *Lord*,
the Maker of *heaven and earth*.

Read it Carefully

Related Verses

"But the Helper, the Holy Spirit whom the Father will send in my name, He will teach you all things, and remind you of all that I said to you."

JOHN 14:26 (NAS)

I can do all this through him who gives me strength.

PHILIPPIANS 4:13

Let us then approach God's throne of grace with confidence, so that we may receive mercy and find grace to help us in our time of need.

HEBREWS 4:16

Study it *Prayerfully*

DO YOU EVER FEEL LIKE you are helping everyone around you, and you wonder who is helping you? As women, we tend to take on so many of the burdens of those around us, that we ourselves can end up feeling overwhelmed, overworked, and underappreciated.

We all need God's help. It's tempting to try to do things on our own and live independently of God, but we will wear ourselves out trying to do it all ourselves. God wants us to surrender our lives to him and be our help in both the good and the bad times.

If you are weary today, pause and look out the window right now. The maker of the sun, moon and stars is with you. He sees all that you are doing, and he loves you. He wants to help you. He never sleeps so you can sleep with peace knowing he is watching over you. When you awake each morning, he is there, and he wants to help carry your burdens. Go to him with every single thing that is burdening you today. You are not alone.

—*Courtney*

> *The Hebrew word for "help" in Psalm 121:1-2 is* **ezer** *(pronounced ay'-zer). Ezer means to protect, surround, aid and help. It is the same word God used to describe Eve when he made a helper for Adam. It also means a strong ally.*

MY **PRAYER** TO **GOD**

Creator God, today I need Your help. Please surround me and protect me and work in the situation of . . .

_____
_____
_____
_____
_____
_____
_____
_____

Live it Out *Practically*

Psalm 121:1-2

I lift up my eyes to the mountains—where does my help come from? My help comes from the Lord, the Maker of heaven and earth.

APPLICATION **QUESTIONS**

Where do you usually turn when you need help? Look out the window right now. What do you see? Are there birds, trees, clouds, or stars?

How does it help to remember that the maker of the heavens and the earth is with you right now? Write out how remembering this increases our faith.

Where I *Saw* God today

Where I *Need* God today

Week 37

CHAPTER OF THE WEEK

Psalm 37

HIGHLIGHTED VERSE

Psalm 37:7

Be *still* before the LORD and *wait* patiently for him; fret not yourself over the one who *prospers* in his way, over the *man* who carries out evil devices! (ESV)

Read it Carefully

Related Verses

Finally, all of you be like-minded and sympathetic, love one another, and be compassionate and humble, not paying back evil for evil or insult for insult but, on the contrary, giving a blessing, since you were called for this, so that you may inherit a blessing.

1 Peter 3:8-9 (CS

See to it that no one repays evil for evil to anyone, but always pursue what is good for one another and for all.

1 Thessalonians 5:15 (CS

Vengeance and retribution belong to me . . .

Deuteronomy 32:35 (CS

Study it *Prayerfully*

Recently, someone in my community was spreading untruths about someone I love deeply. I so badly wanted to correct the errors and protect the name of my loved one and—most importantly—zip the lips of the one spreading lies! It was then that I read Psalm 37:7 and the encouraging words: "Fret not yourself."

I just love that phrase! Now, it isn't one we might normally use in our modern, day-to-day conversations. We are more likely to say something along the lines of, "Don't worry." Or "Try to calm down." But the advice of "Fret not yourself" shows a bit more vividly just what's happening. We are the ones causing ourselves to fret, so perhaps we are the ones who can stop the fretting, too!

When we allow our angry thoughts to become kindling, burning in our minds, they can soon spark angry actions we might regret. We may think we're directing our fiery fury outward, but in fact, we are the ones who end up getting seared and scorched.

Instead, a different approach can bring about a better outcome when we aim to carefully follow the directive in the first part of the verse: Be still. Wait. Display patience—a quiet trust that God is in control. We can focus on controlling our anger and allow God to control the concerning situation, trusting Him with the outcome.

—*Karen*

> *The word "fret" in the Hebrew language of Psalm 37:7 is **charah** (pronounced khaw-raw') and its meaning is "to burn or to be kindled with anger."*

MY **PRAYER** TO **GOD**

Father God, I don't want to take matters into my own hands, but wait for You to act about . . .

_____
_____
_____
_____
_____
_____
_____

Live it Out *Practically*

Psalm 37:7

Be still before the LORD and wait patiently for him; fret not yourself over the one who prospers in his way, over the man who carries out evil devices!

(ESV)

APPLICATION QUESTIONS

If you're worried or troubled today by another's vengeful actions, don't try to fix the outcome or control the situation. Trust God to move, and then give yourself a little three-word pep talk: Fret not yourself.

How can remembering the phrase "Fret not yourself" help you in a situation you are currently facing in life?

What is one action step you can take to acquire more faith and less fret?

Where I *Saw* God today

Where I *Need* God today

Week 38

CHAPTER OF THE WEEK

Romans 5

HIGHLIGHTED VERSES

Romans 5:3-4

We also *glory* in our *sufferings*, because we know that suffering produces *perseverance*; perseverance, *character*; and character, *hope*.

Read it *Carefully*

Related *Verses*

Blessed is the one who perseveres under trial because, having stood the test, that person will receive the crown of life that the Lord has promised to those who love him.

JAMES 1:

Be joyful in hope, patient in affliction, faithful in prayer.

ROMANS 12:

And the God of all grace, who called you to his eternal glory in Christ, after you have suffered a little while, will himself restore you and make you strong, firm and steadfas

1 PETER 5:

Study it *Prayerfully*

ALMOST ALL OF US WOULD AGREE that suffering is the last thing we'd willingly sign up for. The heart-wrenching experience of a miscarriage, the loss of financial security, or struggles with our health are sometimes more than we feel like we can handle. But what if we saw our suffering as a gift?

Romans 5 says, we can "glory" in our suffering. In Greek, the word "glory" isn't just a happy feeling, it means to boast proudly. Think about that for a moment. The apostle Paul is saying we should be proud of the hard things we go through. Imagine you found out tomorrow that you lost your job and you had no idea how you would pay your bills this month. Would you go around and tell everyone about it, boasting about your good fortune? No, probably not! But we can because there is something much deeper going on when we suffer.

Our suffering produces beautiful qualities we need to make it through this life. As we persevere, our character is shaped, and as our character is shaped, we find true and lasting hope. Suffering removes all of the things that steal our focus from what matters most. Our pain purifies our priorities, and our suffering produces lasting fruit.

Whatever you are going through right now, God is at work. Remember that He wants to grow you through your suffering and not just get you through your suffering.

—*Ruth*

> *The word "hope" in Greek,* **elpis** *(pronounced* el-pece'*), means an expectation of good. It is a joyful confidence and trust in God. This is a reminder that what we go through ultimately helps us have trust and confidence in God.*

MY **PRAYER** TO **GOD**

Almighty God, I want the suffering in my life to help me to . . .

_____
_____
_____
_____
_____
_____
_____

Live it Out *Practically*

Romans 5:3-4

We also glory in our sufferings, because we know that suffering produce perseverance; perseverance, character; and character, hope.

APPLICATION QUESTIONS

Is there something you are walking through right now that seems like too much to handle? List it here in the space provided.

How might God be asking you to "glory" in the situation you just described above?

Where I *Saw* God today

Where I *Need* God today

Week 39

CHAPTER OF THE WEEK

Proverbs 10

HIGHLIGHTED VERSE

Proverbs 10:11

The mouth of the *righteous* is a *fountain* of life, but the *mouth* of the *wicked* conceals violence.

Read it Carefully

Related Verses

A good man brings good things out of the good stored up in his heart, and an evil man brings evil things out of the evil stored up in his heart. For the mouth speaks what the heart is full of.

LUKE 6:4

Do not let any unwholesome talk come out of your mouths, but only what is helpful for building others up according to their needs, that it may benefit those who listen.

EPHESIANS 4:2

Out of the same mouth come praise and cursing. My brothers and sisters, this should not be. Can both fresh water and salt water flow from the same spring? My brothers and sisters, can a fig tree bear olives, or a grapevine bear figs? Neither can a salt spring produce fresh water.

JAMES 3:10-

Study it *Prayerfully*

THERE ARE TWO KINDS OF MOUTHS compared in Proverbs. There is the righteous mouth and the wicked mouth. The righteous mouth has words flowing out that are wise and kind and bring life to the hearer. The wicked mouth is harsh and hurts the one who is listening.

How do we get a righteous mouth that is wise and has life flowing from it? We gain wisdom from our walk with God, our life experiences, from having wise mentors, wise friends and from other sources of wisdom like godly podcasts and books.

It does not matter how pretty our hair, make-up or clothes are, it is the words that come out of our mouths that determine our true beauty. How would your friends and family describe the words that come out of your mouth? If you are struggling today, let's be determined to practice self-control with our emotions. When we feel anger bubbling up, sarcasm spilling out or critical remarks being said, these are red flags that the heart needs tended to. Take your frustrations to the Lord and ask him for help to be more gracious, gentler, and a fountain of life to those around you.

—Courtney

> *The Hebrew word for "fountain" in Proverbs 10:11 is* **maqor** *(pronounced* maw-kore'*). Maqor means a well, a spring, a natural source flowing, or a fountain of water.*

MY **PRAYER** TO **GOD**

Maker of my soul, I need to watch my words when it comes to . . .

_____
_____
_____
_____
_____
_____
_____

Live it Out *Practically*

Proverbs 10:11

The mouth of the righteous is a fountain of life, but the mouth of the wicked conceals violence.

APPLICATION **QUESTIONS**

How are you filling your heart with good things so it can overflow onto others? Are you walking with God daily? List what you are currently doing to strengthen your walk with Jesus.

Are you pondering life experiences long enough to gain wisdom from them? Do you have wise mentors and friends? List any that come to mind below.

Finally, are the things that you are reading and watching filled with wisdom? List any that are. Then, list any that are not and draw a line through them. Decide now to only let healthy influences in your life going forward.

Where I *Saw* God today

Where I *Need* God today

Week 40

CHAPTER OF THE WEEK

Colossians 3

HIGHLIGHTED VERSE

Colossians 3:9

And stop *lying* to each other. You have *given up* your old way of life with its *habits*. (CEV)

Read it *Carefully*

Related *Verses*

For the one who wants to love life and to see good days, let him keep his tongue from evil and his lips from speaking deceit, and let him turn away from evil and do what is good. Let him seek peace and pursue it,...

1 PETER 3:10-11 (CS

Lying lips are detestable to the Lord, but faithful people are his delight.

PROVERBS 12:22 (CS

Keep your tongue from evil and your lips from deceitful speech.

PSALM 34:13 (CS

Study it *Prayerfully*

ONE MORNING DURING A SERMON I WAS RATHER ENJOYING, my pastor made a bold statement that pinched my heart just a little. He declared, "People pleasers often lie." Gulp. I had to admit that sadly, there are times I am one fantastic fibber.

Sometimes, I slightly twist the truth so I won't hurt someone's feelings when asked for my opinion. Still in other situations, I outright lie just to avoid a confrontation with someone over a political or other hot-topic issue. And I also admit there are times I only tell half the truth, conveniently leaving parts out. However, as I often tell my children, "A half-truth is still a whole lie."

At the root of all these varied forms of dishonesty is this commonality: I lied in order to please someone else. However, all this twisting, shading, fibbing and half-truth telling certainly does not please the only One who matters—the Lord.

In Colossians 3:9, the Apostle Paul urges believers, "And stop lying to each other. You have given up your old way of life with its habits." Deceit is associated with our behavior before we became followers of Christ. It is not something that should be a character quality of those who've responded to the gospel and become believers.

Thankfully, I know from experience that God can empower us to strip off our dishonest ways, no matter how justified our lies may seem. We can learn to roll our truths in a blanket of love—remembering it is God we seek to please, not others. Let's learn to retrain our brains, not thinking "What do they want me to say?" but instead praying "Lord, help me to speak the truth in love."

—*Karen*

> *The original Greek word for the English phrase "have given up" in Colossians 3:9 is the verb* **apekduomai**. *It is pronounced ap-ek-doo'-om-ahee and it means to strip something completely and emphatically off yourself, to throw something far away. This action is to be performed by the person who is being untruthful.*

MY **PRAYER** TO **GOD**

Father, I desire to be a truth teller, not lying in order to please someone else. Help me to . . .

_____
_____
_____
_____
_____
_____
_____
_____

Live it Out *Practically*

Colossians 3:9

And stop lying to each other. You have given up your old way of life with its habits. (CEV)

APPLICATION QUESTIONS

1 Peter 3:10 declares, "For the Scriptures say, 'If you want to enjoy life and see many happy days, keep your tongue from speaking evil and your lips from telling lies.'" (NLT)

Are you sometimes tempted to shade the truth so you won't upset, disappoint or even anger someone? Name a specific instance where this was the case.

What goal might you make that will help you "keep your tongue from speaking evil and your lips from telling lies"?

Where I *Saw* God today

Where I *Need* God today

Week 41

CHAPTER OF THE WEEK

Psalm 91

HIGHLIGHTED VERSE

Psalm 91:1

Whoever dwells in the *shelter* of the Most High will rest in the *shadow* of the *Almighty*.

Read it *Carefully*

Related *Verses*

May the God of hope fill you with all joy and peace as you trust in him, so that you may overflow with hope by the power of the Holy Spirit.

ROMANS 15:1

It is better to take refuge in the Lord than to trust in humans.

PSALM 118

You came near when I called you, and you said, "Do not fear." You, Lord, took up my case; you redeemed my life.

LAMENTATIONS 3:57-5

Study it *Prayerfully*

WHEN I AM WORRIED AND MY MIND IS RESTLESS, it seems I turn to everything else before God. I clean, I do laundry, I work, I go for a walk, and on and on and on. Anything to get my mind off my present circumstances. Most of the time, I don't even realize I am in this cycle until God nudges me and reminds me that he is there.

I love Psalm 91:1 because it is a promise to us that when we turn to him, we can rest secure. Our minds can stop spinning. And our hearts can stop worrying. In fact, the word "rest" means to abide and remain. This is deeper than a quick rest. This is a quiet confidence and security that we are safe with him.

Do our responses, attitudes, and actions suggest that we are resting in the shadow of the Almighty? God doesn't come close to us to keep us as we are. He calls us and graciously changes us from the inside out. I'm learning ever so slowly to stop, rest, and pray when my heart is heavy. His shelter is safe and secure.

—*Ruth*

> **El-Shaddai**, *(Pronounced el shad-di') or God Almighty, is a name of God meant to communicate His power. We can rest in the shadow of* Shaddai— *the most powerful God. There is no safer place.*

MY PRAYER TO GOD

Father, I need to rest in Your power and stop my mind from spinning about . . .

_____
_____
_____
_____
_____
_____
_____
_____

Live it Out *Practically*

Psalm 91:1

Whoever dwells in the shelter of the Most High will rest in the shadow of the Almighty.

APPLICATION QUESTIONS

How does the image of resting under the shadow of the wings of our powerful God make you feel about your safety?

How does knowing that you can rest under the shelter of the Most High change your approach to today? What specifically will you do differently this week?

Where I *Saw* God today

Where I *Need* God today

Week 42

CHAPTER OF THE WEEK

Philippians 4

HIGHLIGHTED VERSES

Philippians 4:6-7

Do not be *anxious* about anything, but in every situation, by *prayer* and *petition*, with thanksgiving, present your requests to God. And the *peace* of God, which transcends all understanding, will *guard your hearts* and your minds in *Christ Jesus*.

Read it *Carefully*

Related *Verses*

"Therefore I tell you, do not worry about your life, what you will eat or drink; or about your body, what you will wear. Is not life more than food, and the body more than clothes?"

MATTHEW 6:2

But Martha was distracted by all the preparations that had to be made. She came to him and asked, "Lord, don't you care that my sister has left me to do the work by myself? Tell her to help me!" "Martha, Martha," the Lord answered, "you are worried and upset about many things, but few things are needed—or indeed only one. Mary has chosen what is better, and it will not be taken away from her."

LUKE 10:40-4

"Who of you by worrying can add a single hour to your life? Since you cannot do this very little thing, why do you worry about the rest?"

LUKE 12:25-2

Study it *Prayerfully*

LIFE HAS DEALT US ALL A LONG LIST of things that weigh us down. When I am stressed and under pressure, I pretty much crack. Those closest to me have seen this. Sometimes it comes out in tears, sometimes in an overflow of chattiness, sometimes in a temper and other times in a critical spirit.

However, maybe something more is going on inside of us and perhaps it's more than stress.

Sometimes we are battling spiritual attacks and extreme anxiety, worry, bitterness or emotional pain. That is not stress. That is called distress. You see, positive stress can help us accomplish things and energize us to get things done. But negative stress can weigh us down.

God does not want us weighed down, instead he wants us to come to him with all of our burdens, worries and cares and present them to him in prayer. In exchange for all of our burdens, God wants to give us his peace.

—*Courtney*

> *The Greek word for "anxious" in Philippians 4:6-7 is the word* **merimnao** *(pronounced m-er-im-nah'-o). Merimnao means to be apprehensive about, distracted by, or to give careful thought or attention to.*

MY PRAYER TO GOD

Loving Father, sometimes I feel so distracted by the anxiety that weighs upon my heart. When I feel this anxiety well up, help me to . . .

_____

_____

_____

_____

_____

_____

Live it Out *Practically*

Philippians 4:6-7

Do not be anxious about anything, but in every situation, by prayer and petition, with thanksgiving, present your requests to God. And the peace of God, which transcends all understanding, will guard your hearts and your minds in Christ Jesus.

APPLICATION QUESTIONS

Is something distracting you and stealing your peace? List anything you can think of here. Then take it to the Lord now in prayer.

When you are feeling worried or anxious in the future, how can the words of Philippians 4:6-7 help you to respond in confidence?

Where I *Saw* God today

Where I *Need* God today

Week 43

CHAPTER OF THE WEEK

Zephaniah 2

HIGHLIGHTED VERSES

Zephaniah 2:2-3

Seek the Lord, all you humble of the earth, who carry out what he commands. Seek righteousness, seek humility; perhaps you will be concealed on the day of the Lord's anger. (CSB)

Read it *Carefully*

Related *Verses*

If we confess our sins, he is faithful and righteous to forgive us our sins and to cleanse us from all unrighteousness.

1 John 1:9 (CSB)

Therefore, having overlooked the times of ignorance, God now commands all people everywhere to repent.

Acts 17:30 (CSB)

Those whom I [dearly and tenderly] love, I rebuke and discipline [showing them their faults and instructing them]; so be enthusiastic and repent [change your inner self—your old way of thinking, your sinful behavior—seek God's will].

Revelation 3:19 (AMP)

Study it *Prayerfully*

ZEPHANIAH 2 TELLS OF GOD CALLING His people to get their act together because their nation was in a state of disrepair. This prophet—whose name means Yahweh conceals—urges them to repent while there is still time, allowing God to cover and conceal their sins.

The Lord's righteous judgment in this chapter is seen everywhere in the land. Since there is no place to turn where God's judgment will not be present, the people's only hope is to repent. They are able to do this by aligning their behavior with the call outlined in Zephaniah 2:3: "Seek the LORD, all you humble of the land, who do his just commands; seek righteousness; seek humility." What does it look like to seek the Lord? We get a few clues from this verse.

First, we remember that it is the Lord we seek who established the covenant. We don't seek to get our own way; instead, we seek the Lord and his ways. Also, we come in a spirit of humility, not of pride, attempting to live a godly life that seeks to obey the just commands given by God to us. And finally, we remain humble as we go forward, knowing that righteousness is found only in the Lord. If we continually come to him in submission and obedience, he will empower us to walk in humility.

When we do our part by getting ourselves together, God sees our willing hearts. It is then he acts with his incredible power and allows us to be wonderfully renewed.

—*Karen*

> *The Hebrew word for "humble" in Zephaniah 2:3 is* **anavah** *(pronounced* an-aw-vaw'*) and it refers to the meek, lowly, poor, or afflicted.*

MY **PRAYER** TO **GOD**

Father, I need to humble myself low before You now and repent for . . .

_____
_____
_____
_____
_____
_____
_____

Live it Out *Practically*

Zephaniah 2:3

Seek the Lord, all you humble of the earth, who carry out what he commands. Seek righteousness, seek humility; perhaps you will be concealed on the day of the Lord's anger. (CSB)

APPLICATION QUESTIONS

Just as the Lord told wayward people in the Old Testament to gather together and repent, we must get ourselves together—through the power of the Holy Spirit—who can enable us to walk in obedience. We can allow God to do the transforming as we cooperate by humbling ourselves, seeking the Lord and desiring to walk in righteousness by obeying his commands.

Is there an area in your life where you need to seek humility and repentance? Name it here.

In what way do you desire for the Lord to change your heart about this situation?

Where I *Saw* God today

Where I *Need* God today

Week 44

CHAPTER OF THE WEEK

Judges 7

HIGHLIGHTED VERSE

Judges 7:2

The *Lord* said to *Gideon*, "You have too many men. I cannot deliver Midian into their hands, or *Israel* would *boast* against me, 'My own *strength* has saved me.'"

Read it *Carefully*

Related *Verses*

But he said to me, "My grace is sufficient for you, for my power is made perfect in weakness." Therefore I will boast all the more gladly about my weaknesses, so that Christ's power may rest on me. That is why, for Christ's sake, I delight in weaknesses, in insults, in hardships, in persecutions, in difficulties. For when I am weak, then I am strong.

2 CORINTHIANS 12:9-

Have I not commanded you? Be strong and courageous. Do not be afraid; do not be discouraged, for the Lord your God will be with you wherever you go."

JOSHUA 1

For the Lord your God is the one who goes with you to fight for you against your enemies to give you victory.

DEUTERONOMY 20

Study it *Prayerfully*

CAN YOU IMAGINE GOING TO WAR and being told to send your army home? That is exactly what happened to Gideon in the Old Testament times. In Judges 7:2, he was ready to lead the Israelites against one of their enemies, the Midianites, and the task seemed doable with such a great army. Until God told Gideon he wanted him to send most of his army home.

The Israelite army could've won with confidence, but God wanted them to see that ultimately it was his strength that wins wars and not their own. Battles are won by leaning on the strength of the Lord, not won relying on our own skills

At those times when it seems like we are in over our heads, feeling overwhelmed and inadequate, we are exactly where God wants us. At that time, we have no choice but to trust him and cling to his strength and power. And we are in a great position for God to get the glory he deserves.

—*Ruth*

> *The Greek word for "grace" is* **charis** *(pronounced* khar-ece*). It is a word used to describe God's kindness and favor, as well as His strength.*

MY **PRAYER** TO **GOD**

Father God, one place in my life where I need to rely only on Your strength and not mine is . . .

_____
_____
_____
_____
_____
_____
_____

Live it Out *Practically*

Judges 7:2

The Lord said to Gideon, "You have too many men. I cannot deliver Midian into their hands, or Israel would boast against me, 'My own strength has saved me.'"

APPLICATION QUESTIONS

Have you felt ill-prepared, overwhelmed, or unqualified lately? Name any situations where this has been the case.

How can you walk in the strength of the Lord and not on your own in the areas you listed above? What specifically can you do differently to achieve this reliance upon God?

Where I *Saw* God today

Where I *Need* God today

Week 45

CHAPTER OF THE WEEK

Ephesians 2

HIGHLIGHTED VERSE

Ephesians 2:10

For we are his *workmanship*, created in Christ Jesus for *good works*, which God prepared *beforehand*, that we should *walk* in them. (ESV)

Read it *Carefully*

Related *Verses*

I praise you because I am fearfully and wonderfully made; your works are wonderful, know that full well.

PSALM 139:

"You did not choose me, but I chose you and appointed you so that you might go and bear fruit—fruit that will last—and so that whatever you ask in my name the Father will give you.

JOHN 15:1

Therefore, if anyone is in Christ, the new creation has come: The old has gone, the ne is here!

2 CORINTHIANS 5:1

Study it *Prayerfully*

YOU ARE A MASTERPIECE! God created you with a purpose and he loves you so much. You see, we are not saved by our good works, but we were created to do good works. Paul says in Ephesians 2:10, that there are good works that God prepared in advance for us to do. This means that God has a call on your life that is specific. You have been uniquely placed in your family, community, school, job, and church by God.

Are you living your life on purpose? In the game of life, there is no one on the bench. We are all in the game. If your life seems boring or without purpose and you find yourself on social media scrolling and watching other people live their lives, it's time to get off the bench! You are robbing yourself and others of the joy that God has given you, to give to others.

I know it's easy to make excuses to not live on purpose or to think we are not good enough to be used by God. I am a very flawed person; my kids would tell you the same. But despite that, God somehow uses me and he wants to use you too! So, if you know your calling, keep on going! And if you don't, start small today by showing love to the next person you encounter.

—*Courtney*

> *The Greek word for "workmanship" in Ephesians 2:10 is* **poiema** *(pronounced poy'-ay-mah). The word* poiema *is where we get the English word poem. We are God's poem! We are his work of art, only we are not like a statue or sculpture we are more like a song that is active.*

MY **PRAYER** TO GOD

Heavenly Father, I know You have created me for good works. I am Your workmanship! Because of this, I want to . . .

_____
_____
_____
_____
_____
_____
_____

Live it Out *Practically*

Ephesians 2:10

For we are his workmanship, created in Christ Jesus for good works, which God prepared beforehand, that we should walk in them. (ESV)

APPLICATION QUESTIONS

Do you know your purpose? Take a minute to think about your purpose in life and then write out what you believe it to be in the space provided here.

If you have a hard time articulating your purpose, ask God to reveal it to you and begin today by showing love to the next person you see.

Where I *Saw* God today

Where I *Need* God today

Week 46

CHAPTER OF THE WEEK

John 17

HIGHLIGHTED VERSE

John 17:15

I am not *praying* that you take them out of the *world* but that you *protect* them from the *evil one*. (CSB)

Read it Carefully

Related Verses

Therefore, put to death what belongs to your earthly nature: sexual immorality, impurity, lust, evil desire, and greed, which is idolatry.

COLOSSIANS 3:5 (CSB)

Do not be conformed to this age, but be transformed by the renewing of your mind, so that you may discern what is the good, pleasing, and perfect will of God.

ROMANS 12:2 (CSB)

Let the unrighteous go on in unrighteousness; let the filthy still be filthy; let the righteous go on in righteousness; let the holy still be holy." "Look, I am coming soon, and my reward is with me to repay each person according to his work.

REVELATION 22:11-12 (CSB)

Study it *Prayerfully*

HAVE YOU EVER HEARD THE OLD SAYING that asserts, "Christians are to be in the world but not of the world." Two different prepositions are used in this charge: in and of. If you are in something, it refers to your setting—where you are physically located. If you are of something, it means you aren't just near in proximity, but you are an inherent part of it; your very being finds its source in it.

At the close of John 17, we see what has been dubbed the High Priestly Prayer. In this prayer, the Lord addresses the tension that exists in dwelling physically here on earth while also refraining from adopting the mindset, habits, or beliefs of the world. Jesus didn't pray for God to isolate his followers, forming their own exclusive club. He asked God to make them stand out in contrast to the world with regards to their behavior. Just as the bright colored sprinkles on the top of a birthday cupcake stand out from—but are not melted into—the buttercream frosting they are on top of, so believers are sprinkled into the world but are to remain separate from it in behavior.

May the people in our lives observe our set-apart and sanctified ways and desire to know more about the one true God we serve.

—*Karen*

> *The original Greek word "sanctify" used in John 17:17 is **hagiazó** (pronounced hag-ee-ad'-zo) and the definition is to set apart; to be different and consecrated. It also indicates to be pure in stark contrast to things that are profane.*

MY **PRAYER** TO **GOD**

Jesus, I want to be set apart in my behavior. Enable me to . . .

_____
_____
_____
_____
_____
_____
_____

Live it Out *Practically*

John 17:15

I am not praying that you take them out of the world but that you protect them from the evil one. (CSB)

APPLICATION **QUESTIONS**

God, through the Holy Spirit, can empower us to live in this world, rubbing shoulders with those who do not know him, while still being visibly different from them in our moral behavior. He can enable us to live in a way that displays the truth of the gospel to those who are watching us. We do this not only by our actions but also through our verbal interactions with them, as we prayerfully and carefully look for opportunities to share the gospel.

In what relationships in your life do you need to apply the concept of being in the world but not of it?

How can you rub shoulders with those who do not follow Christ, loving them and pointing them to the truth of the gospel?

Where I *Saw* God today

Where I *Need* God today

Week 47

CHAPTER OF THE WEEK

Psalm 23

HIGHLIGHTED VERSES

Psalm 23:1-3

The Lord is my *shepherd*, I lack nothing. He makes me lie down in green *pastures*, he *leads* me beside quiet waters, he *refreshes* my soul. He *guides* me along the *right paths* for his name's sake.

Read it *Carefully*

Related *Verses*

The Lord will guide you always; he will satisfy your needs in a sun-scorched land and will strengthen your frame. You will be like a well-watered garden, like a spring whose waters never fail.

ISAIAH 58:

In their hearts humans plan their course, but the Lord establishes their steps.

PROVERBS 16

The Lord makes firm the steps of the one who delights in him; though he may stumble he will not fall, for the Lord upholds him with his hand.

PSALM 37:23-2

Study it *Prayerfully*

MY FAMILY LOVES TO GO ON WALKS. Sometimes we visit a local nature preserve that isn't quite the typical neighborhood sidewalk we are used to. The trails are steep and windy at times, with lots of roots sticking out, and a time or two, we have almost fallen, navigating our way.

The Bible uses paths as a common metaphor for a relationship with God often. Like our nature preserve path, our life's path isn't always smooth. It sure is nice when it is, but there is a lot more growth when it isn't. We must be more alert and ready for whatever is in front of us.

Psalm 23 says that God leads us like a shepherd down the right path. The path isn't always easy, but no matter how rugged it is, with God, our path leads to life. We tend to search for the easier way, but the Shepherd knows what path is best for us. We can trust him to strengthen our legs and steady our feet for the journey.

—*Ruth*

> *"Leads" in Hebrew is **nahal** (pronounced naw-hal). It means to lead with care, cause to rest and refresh. It is an active guidance by God.*

MY PRAYER TO GOD

Loving Lord, please lead me in Your ways and help me to . . .

_____
_____
_____
_____
_____
_____
_____

Live it Out *Practically*

Psalm 23:1-3

The Lord is my shepherd, I lack nothing. He makes me lie down in green pastures, he leads me beside quiet waters, he refreshes my soul. He guides me along the right paths for his name's sake.

APPLICATION **QUESTIONS**

Has God ever taken you on an unexpected path in the past—one that was totally not anything you'd expected? What happened?

How has God used the different paths in your life to teach you more about Him?

Where I *Saw* God today

Where I *Need* God today

Week 48

CHAPTER OF THE WEEK

Matthew 6

HIGHLIGHTED VERSE

Matthew 6:33

But *seek* first his *kingdom* and his *righteousness*, and all these *things* will be *given* to you as well.

Read it *Carefully*

Related *Verses*

"You shall have no other gods before me."

EXODUS 2

"For where your treasure is, there your heart will be also."

LUKE 12

And without faith it is impossible to please God, because anyone who comes to him must believe that he exists and that he rewards those who earnestly seek him.

HEBREWS 1

Study it *Prayerfully*

JESUS SAID TO SEEK HIS KINGDOM and his righteousness first. This means that he is to be our first priority in life. He should be on our minds first thing in the morning, as we seek his will every single day. But so many days our energy, time and money are spent first on the things of this world and God gets our leftovers. If we have any energy left, then we serve him. If we have any time left, then we seek him and if we have any money left, then we give it to him.

Jesus promises that when we seek him first, he will take care of us but oftentimes what God may think is best for us, may not be exactly what we had in mind. Many times, his timing is slower than ours. And so, seeking God first and trusting God to provide can be hard, especially when we face trials. God does not promise us an easy life. Many believers around the world have been persecuted and died for their faith.

And so, no matter how hard life gets sometimes, we must keep seeking God and his kingdom first. Always remember that we are promised an eternity in heaven with him, where there will be no more pain and no more tears.

—*Courtney*

> *The Greek word for "seek" in Matthew 6:33 is* **zeteo** *(pronounced dzay-teh'-o). Zeteo means to seek after, endeavor or to desire.*

MY PRAYER TO GOD

Dear God, I need to seek Your face when it comes to . . .

_____
_____
_____
_____
_____
_____
_____

Live it Out *Practically*

Matthew 6:33

"But seek first his kingdom and his righteousness, and all these things will be given to you as well."

APPLICATION **QUESTIONS**

What are you seeking after today? Name anything here that you might be tempted to seek after rather than God. Some examples might be money, popularity, or success.

Is there anything you wrote down that is coming before the Lord in your life? Circle it above. Then, next to it write, "I will not seek this any longer. Instead, I will seek the Lord."

Where I *Saw* God today

Where I *Need* God today

Week 49

CHAPTER OF THE WEEK

Psalm 106

HIGHLIGHTED VERSES

Psalm 106:12-13

Then they *believed* his promises and *sang* his praise. But they soon *forgot* what he had done and *did not wait* for his plan to unfold.

Read it *Carefully*

Related *Verses*

"Now, Lord, what do I wait for? My hope is in you.

PSALM 39:7 (CS

Wait for and confidently expect the LORD; Be strong and let your heart take courage, Yes, wait for and confidently expect the LORD.

PSALM 27:14 (AM

But I will look to the LORD; I will wait for the God of my salvation. My God will hear m

MICAH 7:7 (CS

The LORD is good to those who wait [confidently] for Him, To those who seek Him [on the authority of God's word].

LAMENTATIONS 3:25 (AM

Study it *Prayerfully*

SOMETIMES I AM SO IMPATIENT and inquisitive when it comes to what is going on in my life. I want God to tell me what's going to happen next; to explain how my life will unfold. I'd love it if he'd spiritually skywrite the answers to all my whys, hows, and whens.

The ancient Israelites had this same mindset. Sometimes they trusted the Lord and stood on His promises. But they often wobbled and lost their footing. They had to know how. And when. And—most importantly—why?

Psalm 106:12-13 shows us this: "Then they believed his promises and sang his praise. But they soon forgot what he had done and did not wait for his plan to unfold."

Scripture teaches us to believe the promises of God. He is faithful. He has a future full of hope planned for us. He will protect us and provide for us. He knows what he is doing even if at times we are certain he does not. And yes, even at the times when he seems to be silent.

It is God's job to unfold our future. It is our job to trust and glorify him as he does. Let's stop asking him to spiritually skywrite all the answers and let's write his promises on our hearts instead. And then? Let's live like we believe them.

—*Karen*

> *The Hebrew word in Psalms 106:13 for "wait" is* **chakah** *(pronounced khaw-kaw') means to properly await, to adhere to; to a tarry, or to long for.*

MY **PRAYER** TO GOD

Father in heaven, I want to wait for You and trust Your timing about . . .

_____
_____
_____
_____
_____
_____
_____
_____

Live it Out *Practically*

Psalm 106:12-13

Then they believed his promises and sang his praise. But they soon forgot what he had done and did not wait for his plan to unfold.

APPLICATION QUESTIONS

By God not giving us explanations at each turn, it builds our faith. We can go to him prayer asking him to calm our anxious hearts. We can ask him to increase our faith s we aren't consumed by the questions, and help us trust that he—the ever-wise parent—has good in mind for us.

What is one area in life where you wish God would skywrite, telling you exactly what will happen next or what the final outcome will be?

Now, while you wait for the answers to how this situation will unfold, what can you remind yourself that is true about God and his character?

How does remembering the perfect character of God calm your anxious heart?

Where I *Saw* God today

Where I *Need* God today

Week 50

CHAPTER OF THE WEEK

1 Peter 5

HIGHLIGHTED VERSE

1 Peter 5:5

All of you, *clothe* yourselves with *humility* toward one another because, "God opposes the *proud* but shows favor to the *humble*."

Read it *Carefully*

Related *Verses*

Humility is the fear of the Lord; its wages are riches and honor and life.

PROVERBS 2

Do nothing out of selfish ambition or vain conceit. Rather, in humility value others above yourselves, not looking to your own interests but each of you to the interests of the others.

PHILIPPIANS 2:

Therefore, as God's chosen people, holy and dearly loved, clothe yourselves with compassion, kindness, humility, gentleness and patience.

COLOSSIANS 3

Study it *Prayerfully*

WHEN WE START FOLLOWING CHRIST, we are called to put off our old life and put on our new life. This transformation is often referred to in the Bible as a change of clothes. Just like we put on our favorite jacket at the beginning of the day, we are called to clothe ourselves with certain attributes and character qualities.

In 1 Peter 5:5, we are told to dress each day with humility toward one another. Sometimes this is easier said than done. Our pride can creep in, and before we know it, we are looking to our interests and needs instead of others. God uses circumstances in our lives like parenting, work, friendship, marriage, and more to help teach us to live with grace and humility towards those around us.

1 Peter 5:5 is our invitation to practice self-forgetfulness. Furthermore, the humility referred to in this verse has a powerful meaning. There was a particular kind of cape worn by slaves referred to as a tie-up. It showed their servitude. Likewise, we are to wear our humility tied around us so that it is the outward mark and sign and the first thing others notice about us. This is a sincere and sacrificial love for others that we get to live out.

—*Ruth*

> *Be clothed with humility is a Greek verb that means to "tie yourselves up in humility." Like a cloak or a cape, humility is to be gathered tight round about us and tied up so that the wind may not blow it back, nor the rain beat inside it.**

*Taken from Ellicott's *Commentary for Young Readers*

MY **PRAYER** TO **GOD**

Gracious God, I need to tie myself up in humility. Empower me to . . .

_____
_____
_____
_____
_____
_____
_____

Live it Out *Practically*

1 Peter 5:5

All of you, clothe yourselves with humility toward one another because "God opposes the proud but shows favor to the humble."

APPLICATION QUESTIONS

Pride has a sneaky way of working its way into our hearts. In what areas of your life do you need to humble yourself and look to others' interests instead of your own?

How does the image of wrapping yourself up in humility help you to gain this character quality in your life?

Where I *Saw* God today

Where I *Need* God today

Week 51

CHAPTER OF THE WEEK

Isaiah 43

HIGHLIGHTED VERSES

Isaiah 43:1-3

"Do not *fear*, for I have *redeemed* you; I have summoned you by name; you are mine. When you pass through the *waters*, I will be with you; and when you pass through the *rivers*, they will not sweep over you. When you walk through the *fire*, you will not be burned; the *flames* will not set you ablaze. For I am the *Lord* your God, the *Holy* One of Israel, your *Savior*."

Read it *Carefully*

_____
_____
_____
_____
_____
_____
_____
_____
_____
_____
_____
_____
_____
_____
_____
_____

Related *Verses*

Be strong and courageous. Do not be afraid; do not be discouraged, for the Lord your God will be with you wherever you go.

JOSHUA

Even though I walk through the darkest valley, I will fear no evil, for you are with me; your rod and your staff, they comfort me.

PSALM 2

"Peace I leave with you; my peace I give you. I do not give to you as the world gives. not let your hearts be troubled and do not be afraid."

JOHN 14

Study it *Prayerfully*

IN ISAIAH 43, the Lord promises his people that when they go through troubles and trials, he is with them. He knows them by name, and they are his, and so he commands them to not be afraid.

When I went through the darkest season of my life, I printed out these verses and put them beside my bed and I read them over and over until I fell asleep. Many nights that paper was covered with tears until I finally drifted off to sleep. I can testify that God's word is true! I was scared and overwhelmed… but God! He brought me through the deep waters and set my feet on dry ground.

Is something making you fearful today? God knows you by name. You are his. Isn't that comforting? He does not want us living in fear. I know that the trials before you may feel big and scary. It might even feel like you are drowning at times, but God says, he is with you. You can trust him. He will protect you, hold you and care for you. Turn to him with all of your fears and never forget you are precious in his eyes and loved.

—*Courtney*

> *The Hebrew word for "fear" in Isaiah 43:1-3 is* **yare** *(pronounced yaw-ray'). Yare means to be frightened, terrified, or to be in utter dread of.*

MY **PRAYER** TO **GOD**

Lord God, when I feel fear welling up in my soul, help me to remember that Isaiah 43:1-3 says…

_____
_____
_____
_____
_____
_____
_____
_____

Live it Out *Practically*

Isaiah 43:1-3

Do not fear, for I have redeemed you; I have summoned you by name; you are mine. When you pass through the waters, I will be with you; and when you pass through the rivers, they will not sweep over you. When you walk through the fire, you will not be burned; the flames will not set you ablaze. For I am the Lord your God, the Holy One of Israel, your Savior.

APPLICATION QUESTIONS

Is something making you fearful today? List it here.

Isn't it a great comfort to know that through every trial God is with you and he will not let it overwhelm you to the point of ruin? How have you seen God dispel fear in your life before and how does remembering his faithfulness encourage you today?

Where I *Saw* God today

Where I *Need* God today

Week 52

CHAPTER OF THE WEEK

1 Thessalonians

HIGHLIGHTED VERSE

1 Thessalonians 5:14

Encourage the disheartened,
help the weak,
be *patient* with everyone.

Read it *Carefully*

_____
_____
_____
_____
_____
_____
_____
_____
_____
_____
_____
_____
_____
_____
_____
_____
_____

Related *Verses*

And let us consider how we may spur one another on toward love and good deeds, not giving up meeting together, as some are in the habit of doing, but encouraging one another—and all the more as you see the Day approaching.

HEBREWS 10:24-

Each of us should please our neighbors for their good, to build them up.

ROMANS 15

"Greater love has no one than this: to lay down one's life for one's friends."

JOHN 15:

Study it Prayerfully

WHEN I FIRST STARTED FOLLOWING THE LORD in high school, I soon discovered that my old way of living wasn't going to match up with what I was now professing. There were many choices I made that weren't wise as a follower of Christ, and I floundered for a while. But slowly, my eyes were opened, and my heart turned wiser as I learned God's Word and grew in the knowledge of how I was to live.

Even as a Christian over the last almost thirty years, there have been many times where I've found myself floundering because of certain circumstances I was walking through. Walking in faith can be hard, and we will all struggle.

Unfortunately, as Christians, we can be so quick to judge and write off those who seem to be struggling or questioning their faith, but 1 Thessalonians 5:14 is a reminder for us to be patient with everyone. This verse is primarily speaking of the followers of Christ who were struggling to get it right. The disheartened were those that were afraid of persecutions. They were feeling weak because of the circumstances they were walking through, and they needed hope and encouragement. We can be that today to a brother or sister in Christ. God's goodness and mercy are available for all, and we play a part in leading others to him.

—Ruth

> *"Help the weak" isn't referring to physical strength or frailty in general, but rather it refers to those who are not as mature spiritually in conscience so as to discern between right and wrong. They were weak in their faith.*

MY **PRAYER** TO **GOD**

Father, may I be ready and willing to help the weak. Help me to remember...

Live it Out *Practically*

1 Thessalonians 5:14

Encourage the disheartened, help the weak, be patient with everyone.

APPLICATION QUESTIONS

Is there someone in your life with whom you have a hard time displaying patience? Why do you think that you have trouble with this person or situation?

In what ways is God asking you to have more patience with those whom He loves?

Where I *Saw* God today

Where I *Need* God today

Made in the USA
Monee, IL
12 March 2023